The

JESUS

TRILOGY

The

JESUS

TRILOGY

Choice and Will

∞

Beliefs, Emotions, and the Creation of Reality

∞

Love and Surrender

GINA LAKE

Endless Satsang Foundation

www.RadicalHappiness.com

Cover photograph: © iStockPhoto/Philip Cacka

ISBN: 978-1502752727

Copyright © 2014 by Gina Lake

All rights reserved. No part of this book may be used or reproduced by any means, graphic, electronic, or mechanical, including photocopying, recording, taping, or by any information storage retrieval system without the written permission of the publisher except in the case of brief quotations embodied in critical articles and reviews.

Contents

Preface	vii

Choice and Will

Introduction	3
1: The Gift of Free Will	5
2: The Unexamined Life	15
3: The Small Will	23
4: The Software	33
5: The Chooser	43
6: Nothing to Choose	51
7: The Truth	59
8: Living the Truth	71

Beliefs, Emotions, and the Creation of Reality

Introduction	85
1: The Illusory Reality	87
2: The Ego's Reality	101
3: How Beliefs About Yourself Affect Your Reality	113
4: How Beliefs About Others Affect Your Reality	133
5: The Past, the Future, and Now	145
6: A Belief That Takes You Beyond Beliefs	157

Love and Surrender

Introduction	163
1: What Is Surrendered	165
2: Surrendering the "I"	175
3: Surrendering Fear	185
4: Surrendering "I Want"	197
5: Surrendering Knowing	207
6: Surrendering to Love in Relationships	217
About the Author	235

Preface

I, who am known to you as Jesus the Christ, have dictated this trilogy of books for your freedom and enlightenment, and more are forthcoming. They were given in the order in which they appear in this volume, but they can be read in any order.

As for who "I" am, I am the same "I am" that is within each of you. That was my message when I was alive two thousand years ago, and that is my message to you today. The man you knew as Jesus exists today in the dimension from which I am communicating. However, I am no longer a man or even a human, but spirit, as you are as well and as you will know yourself to be after you leave this earth. From the dimension where I exist, I am guiding the planet and am with all who pray to me, because I so deeply love the human race and the earth.

Please understand that, although you knew me as a man who lived in ancient times, the body and personality I had then was merely a costume, just as your own body is a temporary costume. I am not bound to the persona of Jesus of Nazareth, although I often assume this persona when appearing or speaking to people, to comply with their expectations. I exist with some individuality in this dimension but no set persona or personality. Some may find this heretical, but so be it.

The man you knew as Jesus also exists today within each of you in spirit. The consciousness that is behind all life is no different than your own. They are one and the same. Your being is meant to shine as gloriously as I was said to have shone on resurrection day. Resurrection is a metaphor for what is possible within every human being. You are divine.

My purpose is to bring you this very good news: You are divine and, now more than ever before in history, it is possible to realize your divinity, which is to say your loving and peaceful nature. Through simple awareness, inquiry, and a willingness to see the truth, you can become free of all that causes you to suffer and free to create the life you wish to live, which is the life the Father wishes for you as well. You are meant to be happy, and the willingness to explore and expose the false and limiting beliefs that keep you suffering and imprisoned is the key to your divinity and to everything you need to be happy.

I am speaking to you through this author because she has the ability to transmit my words and because she has been devoted to me in many lifetimes as a religious person. However, you do not have to be religious or devoted to me to benefit from these teachings. You simply need to be open to investigating the mystery of who you are.

I have not used Christian terminology in particular, because I am not a Christian or a Jew or a Muslim or a Hindu, nor do I belong to any other religion or sect. I represent and have always represented the Consciousness within you. I reflected the Love that you are so that you could know it within you. That was my purpose. I did not come to be worshipped but to show you the way to love and worship all of life.

Some will call this message new age, but there is nothing new about it. It is the message of everyone who has realized Christ Consciousness within themselves, which you will do one day as well, if you haven't already. Please do not put a label on this message, as any label only causes separation, and my intent is to unite, not separate.

My message was always one of peace, not separation, and this is my message now. Peace on earth will not come from seeing yourself as a Christian, a Jew, a Muslim, a Hindu, or anything else, but by seeing yourself as you truly are, as I see you and know you, as the Father sees and knows you. When you can see the face of God in your neighbor and love and care for your neighbor as you would yourself, then peace will come to earth. Any belief that interferes with that must go. It is time now to live in harmony with each other.

Some may say that these teachings are not the same as the ones I gave long ago. But these teachings are the ones I would give today if I were alive, and they are in words that I might use today. In the past, my voice and language was the voice and language of those times. For now, this is the voice and language I am choosing to use.

In the past, my teachings had to be couched in parables, but today they can be plainly spoken. The world is a very different place, and the culture you live in is a very different one. More importantly, consciousness has evolved and is finally ready for these words. In the past, these teachings were for the few who might benefit. Now many can gain from them. So, I offer them to all who are willing to consider them. May they carry you more speedily to the peace and love you so long for and deserve.

Book I

Choice and Will

Introduction

In this first book, we will explore the mystery of choice and will. In the spiritual journey from being imprisoned by your conditioning to being free, or fully enlightened, choice and will play a key role. The road to enlightenment is marked by an evolving relationship to the issue of choice and will. Where initially, one's free will is subsumed by conditioning and people stray little from their conditioning, as spiritual evolution progresses, people learn to use their will in a way that increases their peace and happiness and lessens their suffering. With further progress, one's free will becomes indistinguishable from divine will, or Thy will. At that point, it is difficult to talk about will at all, because choosing is effortless and just happens without a sense of choosing. What is there to choose against when there is no longer a personal will in conflict with divine will?

Some of you may be interested in reading this because I, Jesus, have dictated it, while others may reject it for the same reason. However, the authorship is not the point. Choosing to believe or not believe that I am behind this book is not as significant as whether you choose to believe the words in it. That choice is much more important, because that choice could be transformative.

You are here deciding whether or not to continue reading, so what will make that choice? What is choosing to continue even now and what will choose to continue or not in the next moment? And what might cause you to put the book down? A judgment?

A belief? A conclusion? A feeling? Where did that come from, and is that a good guide for making your choice? Can you trust that? Do you trust that?

What is the basis for your choices? How do you know what to choose? This is the mystery we will explore together. You have been given the great gift of free will. How will you use it? The answer to that question determines your experience of life.

Jesus, dictated to Gina Lake
November, 2013

Chapter 1

The Gift of Free Will

You have been given the gift of free will. This gift requires one thing: consciousness. By consciousness, I mean awareness of the possibility of choice. Without this awareness, human beings would not be very different from animals, who function and survive primarily through instinct and other conditioning. Similarly, if you are not aware that you have a choice and if you don't exercise it, you also will function mostly according to your instincts and conditioning.

Human beings, like animals, are born with software, to use a metaphor, which largely determines how they respond to life. This software is designed to optimize survival but not other things essential to human beings, such as love, peace, happiness, and fulfillment. In fact, this software often interferes with achieving happiness and fulfillment.

This software is primitive, although it has some functionality. It is useful in its proper domain, which is survival, but ineffectual and even counterproductive outside that domain. For instance, if you see a forest fire, this software motivates you to flee from the fire. However, when faced with the stresses of modern life, that same programming might cause you to flee your responsibilities or behave badly in your relationships. Fight or flight is a functional response only for issues related to survival.

Fear is useful in responding to *immediate* threats to physical safety. It is not useful in dealing with the ordinary demands, including survival issues, of modern life, when fear is counterproductive. If you rely on your software to determine your responses to nonlife-threatening circumstances, your responses will be governed by the primitive, programmed, part of yourself, which is often called *the ego*.

The ego is the software that gives you the sense that you are "in here," inside your body, and everything else is "out there," outside of and separate from you. The ego makes you feel alone and vulnerable to harm from others and life in general. You feel like "it's me against the world."

The ego also makes it seem like you are your body and your mind. It seems like who you are is the body and the thinker of the thoughts that go through your mind. However, this is hardly an adequate description of who you are. Your body and your mind are "yours," after all, so who is this *you* to which the body and mind belong?

While something experiences the body and something experiences thinking, there is actually nobody who is thinking those thoughts. Thinking is happening, but it isn't happening to somebody or being done by somebody. You cannot find a *who* that thinking is happening to. It is just happening. If you argue, "Well, *I* am thinking," then who is this *I*? You cannot find it. It is just a concept of *I*. It is just a thought about *I*.

This truth is a bit obscure, but you can discover it for yourself by simply looking to see if there is someone in there who is thinking and by looking to see where your thoughts come from. When you investigate, you discover that who you think you are is not as tangible as you may have believed.

The ego, or the programmed self, creates a sense of self and an identity from the thoughts about yourself. The sense of self created by the ego is often called the *false self* to distinguish it from your true nature. It is false because it doesn't actually exist beyond thoughts about yourself. All the false self is, is thoughts about yourself.

These thoughts tell you who you are, and you declare this to others: "I do not like green eggs and ham!" People rarely question their thoughts, where they come from, and if they are even true. They accept their mind's description of themselves and hone this description daily with new information: "I do so like green eggs and ham." (from the popular children's book, *Green Eggs and Ham,* by Dr. Seuss)

This description of yourself is always changing to fit new information and experiences, but who is it that updates this information? Are you even aware of your ideas about yourself being updated? And do you always agree with the description? Who is it that can even observe this process? It seems that there is someone or something shaping the description and someone or something who is aware of this description and can agree or disagree with it. That's interesting. Which one are you?

It is as if there is a computer taking in information, processing it, and updating your self-images, like updates to your software. In fact, that is what the brain is. It is a computer that stores, processes, and accesses information. The information that goes into this computer comes from many different sources, which is why the information is sometimes contradictory and might even be false.

The brain records information, but it doesn't have the wisdom to evaluate it: garbage in, garbage out, as the saying goes. When the brain does evaluate information, it does so based on other stored information. This process can hardly pass as wisdom, although it often does.

Fortunately, something else does have wisdom, although what that is, is rather mysterious. So, what is going on here? The brain stores and processes information, but you are much more than this computer-mind, aren't you? Isn't it more likely that you are what is able to be aware of and bring wisdom to the information that your brain and other brains have processed?

This ability to be conscious of and think about thoughts distinguishes human beings from animals, whose ability to do this is rudimentary. And this is where free will comes in. You not only have the ability to be conscious of your thoughts—your software—but also the ability to *choose* what you think, that is, what you believe and how you define yourself! Moreover, you have the ability to choose how you will respond to your thoughts. In other words, unlike animals, you can override your software if you choose. This allows human beings to evolve by leaps and bounds, far beyond the ability that any other creature has to evolve.

Through this amazing ability to choose, you become a co-creator with Life. Free will makes it possible for you to co-create with Life! What an amazing gift that is! You get to try your hand at shaping life alongside Life itself. There is little in life that is quite as exhilarating and fun as creating.

Your ability to create, including making art, telling stories, composing music, writing books, producing machines and new products, building institutions, uncovering new information, developing technology, designing and engineering structures, and discovering new medicines, sets you apart from the rest of creation. The ability to override and operate beyond your instincts and the rest of your software—this gift of free will—is responsible for so many wonderful creations.

Free will also allows you to become a destroyer of life. Free will even allows that. It allows you to destroy life, destroy love, destroy peace, and destroy your happiness. It allows you to be hateful, make war, be greedy, damage your environment, and be afraid. It allows you to make choices that lead to terrible outcomes. So, free will comes at a cost: To enjoy the benefits of it, you will also suffer the effects until you learn to use your will more wisely.

From the standpoint of the Infinite, because the Infinite honors free will and because it gave you this gift, no choice is ever considered wrong or bad. However, some choices lead to better outcomes than others. So, to say that there are no wrong choices does not mean that there are not paths that are best not taken. But it is often difficult to know this about a choice beforehand.

Through trial and error, you discover what is true and not true for you, what is beneficial and wise, and what is not. And even so-called bad or unpleasant outcomes can be appreciated for the inner gifts they bestow, such as courage, perseverance, wisdom, strength, patience, and compassion.

The benevolence of life is such that no matter what you choose, that choice will contribute to your evolution. Suffering ensures that, and this is how it works: Evolution has a certain trajectory: It goes toward love. If your choices take you away from love, you suffer. That suffering will inevitably put you back on course. You get to choose, of course, how long that will take.

Because suffering serves a purpose in pointing you toward Home, even suffering is a gift. Every choice either celebrates life and furthers creation or shows you the unworthiness of that choice and, in so doing, furthers your understanding.

The choices that lead to suffering *always* teach you something—usually a number of things. You may not realize what you have learned or be able to put that into words, but through every choice you make, life teaches you—it changes you. The choices that lead to the most suffering often reap the most gifts, the greatest learning.

What is learned by suffering? At the very least, compassion. That is no small thing and not likely to be learned through other means. Empathy and compassion are only the beginning, however, for they naturally, although not immediately, flower into a desire to relieve suffering in others. Everyone who finds joy in serving others has no doubt suffered greatly in this lifetime or in others.

Service is love, is it not? Love is identification with another as one's own self. Giving to others as you would like to be given to naturally flows from this identification with others. Love is one of the sweetest fruits of suffering.

Furthermore, if the experience of suffering is investigated, it will reveal the real cause of suffering, and that wisdom is an immeasurably valuable prize. The seeds of freedom are within the very thing that seems to imprison.

Love is inescapable. If you fail to love, you feel the pain of a closed heart. That suffering underlines the importance of love, and so you seek love. That seeking eventually leads to finding love—to learning to love. Through every little act of love, you make your way Home. Whatever you choose, even choosing not to love, moves you closer to love and ultimately to your enlightenment.

You cannot help but become enlightened. With every act of love, you become lighter, more filled with light, as the darkness is cast out. What is this darkness? It is ignorance of the Light: ignoring the Light while giving attention to something else. The darkness is nothing, really. It doesn't exist but is merely the seeming absence of something that *does* exist: Light.

What is Light? Light is another word for Love, for the energy of and behind all life. There is nothing but Light. It is the substance, the underlying ground of being, of which the universe—creation—is composed and from which everything is born.

The only thing that can obscure the Light is acknowledging something else instead. This is a choice, of course. You are free to choose to acknowledge the truth of your unity with all creation or to acknowledge the sense of separateness, fear, and alienation, which are the byproducts of your software. Ignorance is believing that your software accurately represents the truth about who you are and about reality. Enlightenment is knowing the truth about who you are and about reality—and living that truth.

Most human beings are in a prison of sorts. It is a prison created by seeing themselves and life as their thoughts describe, without realizing that their thoughts do not accurately represent reality. People who live in this prison do not question their thoughts and are not even particularly aware of them. They respond to their thoughts as if under a spell, as if commanded to follow them, as if they have no free will. They are like puppets, with their software pulling the strings, asleep to life, asleep to reality. They are living an unexamined life.

This creates a hell on earth, because the software is not simply stored information; it is corrupted with lies, fear, selfishness, and limiting beliefs. The software keeps people prisoners of their own fear, prisoners of lies, and prisoners of their own base emotions. There is little chance of happiness for those who respond so unthinkingly to their software, only suffering.

Many remain imprisoned, angry, feeling victimized, and blaming others for their pain without realizing that they are their own jailor and their own persecutor. Their own minds are the cause of their pain and ill-doing! Suffering will eventually lead to their release but often not until they have brought more suffering to themselves and others. This would be a sorry state if there were no keys to this prison. The key is, in fact, free will. Free will allows people to stay in prison if they are choosing that, however unconscious that choice might be, *and* free will offers the possibility of freedom.

The software is not even the problem, as some aspects of it are useful. The problem is not realizing the software's limitations and believing it can do more than it was designed to do. Expecting your software to be capable of defining you and providing a philosophy by which to create a happy, peaceful, and loving life is like expecting your computer to be able to do those things for you. Looking to your thoughts for how to live your life is not much better than asking one of those Magic 8 fortunetelling balls that you had as a child what to do.

Computers are not wise; they only store and process information. Your thoughts are not wise; they only reflect the information that you and others have acquired. Information is useful in its proper place, but information is not enough to guide you in this vast mystery called life. You are so much more than the information stored in your brains and so much more than what your thoughts tell you that you are. And yet, the software is so often what is running people's lives. It is taken as the master when it is only a servant.

The situation is made worse because the software promulgates and maintains the ego's perspective, which is one of fear, lack, and self-centeredness. That is where the great deception and the suffering begin. The ego paints a picture of reality that is far from reality. It presents a philosophy or perspective that is anti-life and anti-love. When you follow such a philosophy, it has to lead to suffering, because how else will you discover the falseness of those beliefs and return to love?

This situation is remedied by using your free will to see that the software is only software and that something else is available to guide life. You use your will to wake up from the domination of the programming, and then you use your will to make more conscious choices about what you will believe, how you will behave, and what you will do.

An enlightened being is one who is free from the limitations of the software, who creates life according to a different will than the programming, a greater will: Thy will. When the programming of the puppet-self is no longer allowed to dominate and shape life, what is left is simply Life living itself. When that happens, only Thy will remains. When only Thy will remains, very little sense of having a will exists, only choosing that happens naturally without any conflict, confusion, or suffering, since those were merely byproducts of the software.

Chapter 2

The Unexamined Life

Everyone has free will, but there's a catch: your software. Because your software is capable enough of keeping you alive, you don't need to exercise free will to stay alive. From the standpoint of your animal nature, free will is an unnecessary luxury. Your software allows you to operate on autopilot, so to speak. It steers you with its thoughts, desires, and aversions. Unfortunately, although your software is enough to maintain life, it is not enough to have the happy, fulfilling, peaceful, and creative life that human beings long for beyond merely surviving.

The extent to which you will have a happy and fulfilling life depends on your exercise of free will. However, there is a catch to that as well, as exercising free will can just as well bring suffering and unhappiness until you learn to choose wisely.

Given this, the course of human evolution generally goes like this: People adhere to their software, then they begin to exercise more free will and create a lot of suffering (as did their software), and then they learn to be happy and at peace. They go from being a human animal to being a mistaken human to being an enlightened human.

When your software is guiding your life, it feels like you have free will because you feel yourself making choices. But what are those choices based on? What is your basis for choosing? The basis is the programming, the conditioning. You may feel like you are choosing, but your software is actually choosing for you, for until your thoughts have been examined and questioned, your thoughts are what run your life.

You may think you are running your life, but if you haven't examined your beliefs, fears, assumptions, conclusions, desires, and aversions, then they will determine your choices and therefore your experience of life. Your thoughts lead to predictable, almost preordained, choices, which result in somewhat predictable experiences and outcomes.

You may think your experience of life is how life actually is, but you create your experience of life by what you believe and what you do. You think a certain way or do something, and those around you respond accordingly. You may not be aware of how your beliefs or behavior shape other people's responses to you, but they do. When you are nice, others are nice; when you are unkind, others are unkind; when you are angry, others are angry; when you think badly of yourself, others think badly of you. Others mirror you back to yourself, at least much of the time.

Even if others don't comply with this shaping, how you react internally to whatever is happening determines your experience of life. For instance, if someone responds angrily to some kindness of yours, you can create the internal experience of forgiving them or the internal experience of feeling angry or victimized by them. You get to choose, although you might not be aware that you have a choice or feel you have one. In this way, you create your experience of life, if not your external experience by shaping it, then certainly your internal experience by how you choose to perceive whatever is happening.

When people do not question their thinking, which is the case when their software is running them, they are not free and their will is not free. Their free will is strangled by the programming, and they are caught in a groove of reacting without questioning those reactions. For example, if you don't question your thoughts, then you'll probably react angrily whenever someone is angry with you, without realizing you have a choice, even though being angry doesn't feel good.

This reaction is understandable, since anger is part of the fight or flight programming of the human animal and is therefore an automatic response in the face of what seems to be a threat. If you get angry often enough, that response feels all the more natural and right, in its own way. The more often you respond angrily to situations, the easier it is to respond that way, because that programming has been reinforced. The groove has gotten deeper. Getting out of that groove will take awareness and a conscious choice to do so.

If certain behaviors are repeated often enough, they become automatic and even addictive. The feeling of being compelled to act a certain way and having no choice about it is how the unexamined life feels much of the time. People feel compelled to respond the way they usually respond, as if there is no other choice. Their thoughts and feelings tell them to respond a certain way, and they believe their thoughts and feelings are what is true for them, even though the results are unpleasant. Because they don't examine their thinking, they don't consider responding any other way.

Life is very difficult, indeed, for those who do not examine their thoughts. They experience so much suffering and no way out, since the only way out would be to become aware of their thoughts and question them. They don't realize that they are the one creating their suffering because they trust something that does not deserve their trust—their thoughts. They trust something to guide their life that is not up to the task.

In a way, those who are so deeply in the grip of their conditioning are not responsible for what they do. They have given over control of their choices to the primitive aspect of themselves, the ego. They follow the dictates of their conditioned mind and the minds of others without questioning or examining their choices, without even seeing that they have a choice. They have fooled themselves into thinking that they are making choices, when in reality they are being controlled by the ego, by the thoughts that run through their mind. They are not exercising their free will.

"Forgive them for they know not what they do" applies to so many across the planet, who have not yet recognized their inherent right and responsibility to consciously choose their responses to life. And yet, life *will* hold them accountable by creating circumstances that will demonstrate to them the power they have to shape reality, which they have been endowed with through the gift of free will.

When the will has been subsumed or taken over by the software, then life is being run by what I will call the *small will* or *my will,* as opposed to *Thy will.* The funny thing is that what people think of as *my will* is, in most cases, not free will at all but the will of the software, of the human animal. It is the will of the ego.

Something needs to happen to break out of such automatic and often dysfunctional programmed responses. The will to choose differently needs to be awakened. But how does that come about? How is the will to go against one's conditioning ignited or developed? The only reason one would choose differently than the software is if the results were unpleasant or undesirable—and if you were not willing to accept those results.

If living the programmed life worked and was satisfying, then everyone would keep living that way. But the programming doesn't deliver the peace, happiness, and love that everyone longs for. Instead, it delivers suffering. That is the bad news, but it is also the good news. This suffering is the prod that wakes people up out of the trance of ego domination and awakens free will, although many endure suffering for a very long time before waking up.

How long suffering continues depends in part on how effectively the conditioning itself keeps one from seeing a way out of that suffering. For example, if you were taught that suffering is everyone's lot in life or if you were conditioned to believe that you deserve to suffer, you might never seek a way out. Or if you are busy blaming others for your suffering, you aren't likely to discover the real cause of it.

The ego copes with suffering by blaming others, giving up and playing the victim, accumulating material possessions, overindulging in sensual pleasures and escapist activities, or trying to become successful, wealthy, famous, beautiful, or anything else that the ego believes will deliver happiness. Of course none of these coping mechanisms works for very long because such strategies do not address the root cause of suffering.

Is there a way out of suffering? At some point, this question dawns and, if pursued, will eventually lead to freedom from suffering, because the answer is yes! You were never meant to suffer endlessly but to realize the truth about your suffering and then wake up out of it. That is how benevolent Life is. It wakes you up out of the nightmare produced by your software, and it does this most effectively through suffering.

When going along with the ego's choices turns out badly, as it so often does, people begin to see through the illusion: Thoughts are not always true and wise. The *I* that is represented by thoughts is not so smart after all! It makes a lot of poor choices and causes a lot of suffering. It talks a good game, but the results cannot be counted on. This is extremely humbling to admit, which is why acknowledging this can take so long.

The thoughts that run through your mind were never intended to run the show, nor are they needed to run the show. This software, which includes the ego, is just a tool and quite an outdated one for the modern world. It serves survival and nothing more.

Many see that the thoughts that run through their mind are not what they pretend to be, and so they try to fix their thoughts. They try to get better, smarter, and more positive thoughts. But a tool will always be just a tool. You can create a more positive ego, but the ego will still be an ego. The creativity, love, peace, and wisdom of your true nature—the vitality behind all life—does not flow from your ego. Creativity, love, peace, and wisdom cannot be found there, in the thoughts that run through your mind.

The only way out of the predicament of having thoughts that are not wise but pretend to be is to stop allowing such thoughts to run your life and to put something else in charge instead. The ego's replacement is not hard to find. It is the very thing that realizes the need to replace the ego. It has been present all along, although dormant to some extent, waiting for you to notice that you have a choice and waiting for you to notice *it*. Until then, life remains largely unexamined.

The unexamined life may not seem unexamined, however, because it is highly examined by the mind itself—by the ego. The mind, in fact, obsesses about *I, me, mine* and particularly about *my life*. This obsession with ideas about oneself and one's life is quite the opposite of examination—those ideas themselves need to be questioned. Thinking about *me* and examining *my life* only reinforces the conditioned self and does nothing to deconstruct or see through the conditioning. The examination needs to come from something beyond the conditioned mind, and many people do not even consider that there is such a thing.

The mind also carefully examines its choices, deliberating over the pros and cons before coming to a decision. Surely, such a rational decision-making process could pass as examination! However, in making decisions this way, the mind is simply sifting through the information in the computer and making choices based on conditioning, including what happened in the past and what it believes will happen in the future.

This information is somewhat useful, but too much is expected of the thinking mind. These thoughts are presumed to be what they are not: wise guides for how to live your life. If you examine the mind for answers to how to live your life, you will get answers, but they will be the conditioned mind's answers. You are still operating in the mind's world. You are still in the domain of the software.

These thoughts about yourself are assumed to represent who you are and what you believe and stand for. But do they? Do your thoughts represent who you are, or do they represent a character that you call yourself, that you define yourself as, that you see yourself as, and perhaps that others see you as? Is that who you are? Is that even who you want to be? And who is it that might want to be different?

Most people do not want to be who their thoughts describe themselves to be. Many people believe that one way to be more like what they want to be like is to have more positive thoughts. So, they try to redesign their thoughts and self-images to reflect what they think they would like to be. But according to whom? According to whose values?

For the most part, people want to be and be seen as smarter, more attractive, richer, more successful, and more competent than someone else, because these things put them on the top of the heap, ahead of the game. But it is only the ego that wants to be and be seen in these ways. This is just the ego doing the self-improvement thing. The ego tries to improve itself for the same reason it does everything else: to survive better, to get what it wants, and to be better than others.

What is rarely appreciated is that even achieving these things can be a source of suffering, because you can never be smart enough, attractive enough, rich enough, successful enough, or competent enough to satisfy the ego. Whatever you accomplish, it is never enough for the ego. The game is rigged. You never arrive at these or any of the ego's goals, at least not for long, even if these things would be enough to bring lasting peace and happiness, which they aren't.

The real issue is, what is this self that is being improved upon? Isn't it just an image of yourself? Aren't you just trying to improve the character that you are playing—your image? Aren't you more than this character? What are you, anyway? Who are you? And who do you want to be? And who is it that wants to be something? These are the questions that make for an examined life. These questions hold the keys to the prison of the unexamined life, the keys that open the door to the possibility of a life without suffering.

What do I mean by a life without suffering? The mind imagines this to be a life in which every one of its desires is met to its fullest. But that would not be a life without suffering and that is not even within the bounds of reality. What I mean is that it is possible to experience life and all its challenges, indeed hardships, with peace, acceptance, and grace, without closing your heart to life and without feeling angry or victimized by the vicissitudes of life.

How is this possible? It is only possible through a transformation of your relationship to your thoughts, a transformation of perspective: You begin to see out of the eyes of your true being rather than out of the eyes of the ego. This transformation is happening every day to many, many people. And, if it hasn't happened to you already, it is happening to you right now.

Chapter 3

The Small Will

I am calling the ego's will small, not because it is not powerful, but because there exists a greater will within which the ego's will operates, although the ego is not aware of this greater will, what I will call Thy will or divine will.

Whether the ego is not aware of divine will or whether it just doesn't trust it matters little, as the result is the same: The ego rejects the possibility that something wiser than it is in charge. The ego doesn't see or doesn't wish to see that it is not the center of the universe and that its will is not supreme. So, you cannot count on the ego to point you to this great mystery at the core of life, only away from it.

The ego distracts you from noticing that a greater will exists by presenting you with its will as a replacement and confidently touting its benefits: "Follow me, and you'll be happy," it says. "Follow my beliefs, ideas, fantasies, desires, drives, and goals, and you will attain happiness. Believe my fears, and that will keep you safe," it promises. Its certainty is convincing. But what the ego claims is a lie.

I am anthropomorphizing the ego to make a point. But I'm justified in doing so, because the ego anthropomorphizes itself as a way of making itself real. The ego is not actually an entity or a thing, although it seems like one. The ego is an illusion, because the ego is not what it appears to be, although it is something. What it is, is programming that makes *you* feel like an entity, an individual, as opposed to merged with the Oneness, which is actually the case.

Without this sense of separation from the Oneness, the Oneness could not have the delicious experience of itself in the various forms of creation. What a delight it is to experience itself as every creation! What better way for the Oneness to enjoy its handiwork!

Human beings are special and especially dear to the Oneness, as they are also creators, more so than any other animal, because human beings have sentience, or knowledge of themselves. Without this sense of themselves and the ability to think about themselves and about life, human beings would not create as they do.

To achieve this sentience, it was necessary to create an ego. The sense that the ego provides of being an individual creator and actor in life is not a problem and doesn't in and of itself cause suffering. The ego serves creation. Nor is fear, for which the ego is responsible, necessarily the cause of suffering, since fear has some value for survival.

The real cause of suffering is that this primitive aspect of the self—the ego—has taken prominence over the true self, which is relatively asleep in most people. The ego pretends to be the king of consciousness, but it is not wise enough to be a king. Like anyone who is not up to a task, the ego is bound to fail miserably at being king. And so it does.

The failure of the ego to create the happiness it promises causes a great deal of suffering. People jump through hoops to follow the ego's prescription for happiness, while never being able to attain lasting happiness. They are set up by the ego to fail. However, the worst sort of suffering is caused by believing that the ego's perspective on life is the truth. The ego sees through a lens of fear, distrust, lack, judgments, and limiting beliefs, which are at the root of all negative feelings and ultimately behind all the harmful and hurtful acts on this planet. And sadly, the ego causes people to overlook the beauty, bounty, and benevolence of life and the value and preeminence of love and peace.

The drama created by the ego pretending to be king has been a rightful part of the evolution of the human species. So much has been learned and experienced by the mischief created by the ego! But now it is time for this phase of human evolution to come to a close and for your true self to awaken from its slumber and take its rightful place on the throne of your consciousness. It is time, and this is why so many are speaking of these truths now.

Awakening begins by stripping away the illusion that has masked the truth for so long. To accomplish this, we need to take a close look at the ego, or *false self*. This term reflects the situation well, as the ego seems like a self and may even seem like your true self, but this is an illusion—false. The ego is neither a self nor the true self.

The ego is programming that makes it appear that your thoughts represent who you are. However, the self that is portrayed by your thoughts is just a concept about who you are, nothing more than that. These thoughts do not point to anything real, although something much more real than this concept of *you* exists, or you wouldn't be able to read these words. It is just that this mystery that you are is not like anything else you experience with your mind and senses, because who you really are is beyond your mind and senses. It is what is using them.

The concept of *you* is constructed from ideas about what you like and don't like, what you want and don't want, what you believe and don't believe, what happened to you in the past, and what you want and don't want to happen to you in the future. There are other ideas that make up *you*, but these are the most common types of thoughts that give *you* a sense of solidity, of being somebody with a storyline. These thoughts make you feel like someone who has a life, which is also just a concept.

Like the idea of *you*, the idea of your life is just a story. This story is not a universal one, however, since other people have their own stories about you. The story of you and your life takes place only in your head.

Your mind is very busy maintaining and molding this sense of you and updating the story of your life. The story of you and your life is shaped and re-shaped moment to moment. In one moment, you are a winner, and in another, you are a loser. Sometimes your life is great, and sometimes it is terrible.

The story is never that unique or original. The story *du jour* is based on whether or not you are getting what you want. You are happy when you get what you want and unhappy when you don't. Only the details change: "I got the job! Now I won't ever have to worry about money. My baby was born. Now everything will be perfect. I broke up with my boyfriend. Now my life will be miserable."

Stories are essentially conclusions told from the ego's perspective. But what conclusion could ever be true about this ever-unfolding, multifaceted, and ineffable mystery called life? Life is too big for the ego to comprehend, so it tries to bring life down to size by telling a story and putting itself at the center of that story. But such a small story, because it captures so little of the truth, can only beget suffering.

The stories the mind tells have an insidious side. They are not just simplistic and unreliable but calculated to pose a problem that needs to be solved, because that is how the ego keeps the false self alive. The mind's stories are usually about something that is lacking or not right and needs fixing, according to the ego. So, on to the next self-improvement project!

If you felt complete and at peace, there would be no self to fix! No, the ego's goal is not for you to become enlightened, for then the ego would cease to be in command. The ego would lose control, because you would see that you didn't need the ego, and then it would fall into the background, where it belongs. The ego frames life experience in the way that it does because doing so keeps the sense of self and the desires that drive the self alive.

Desires both define the false self and drive it toward goals that the ego and one's conditioning deem worthy, such as acquiring more material possessions, achieving success, becoming recognized, having financial security, and being comfortable and safe. Most people don't question these desires and goals. They seem to be what life is all about and what is necessary for happiness. Pursuing these goals seems perfectly natural and desirable, if only because doing so is so normal.

Such desires and goals *are* natural, and nothing is wrong with having them or achieving them. They lead to the many rich experiences you have as human beings. However, longing for something you don't have is painful, and achieving the ego's goals doesn't deliver the happiness that is promised, but only leads to more desires, more striving, and consequently more suffering. But since everyone seems to be suffering, this also seems normal. And so the life the ego creates and the resulting suffering is not questioned.

The desires, goals, and suffering of the ego are so universal and deeply established that it is difficult to imagine life being any other way. From this perspective, it seems that the only way to improve your life and become happier is to keep refining your desires and goals and keep trying to achieve them: If that last achievement didn't do it for you, then you try for a higher or different achievement.

Achieving the ego's goals is what the small will is all about. The ego can accomplish so much when it puts its mind to it. Willpower can be used to lose weight, to stay up all night and cram for a test, to win a race, to push yourself to do anything. The small will is there for the harnessing. Nevertheless, some limiting bit of conditioning, some belief or habit, often sabotages people's best intentions.

If only willpower could be harnessed *at will!* But the small will is easily undermined, because it is not one-pointed but pointed in many directions at once. The small will is directed by desires, and the ego's desires are all over the place. Hence, the self-sabotage: You want to ace the test *and* you want to sleep; you want to lose weight *and* you want to eat dessert; you want to win that race *and* you want to do other things. The boat that is manned by the ego is a rudderless one: It goes this way and that way.

The small will can be made one-pointed through focus, which many have learned to do. If your attention is focused on achieving a particular goal to the exclusion of all others, you have a good chance of getting what you want. This is the secret that many with so-called willpower have learned.

More important than focus, however, is whether your goal is worth your undivided attention. Maybe it is. But often it is not. Most people's goals are arbitrary, superficial, or belong to someone else. When that is the case, mustering willpower to accomplish that goal will be difficult. And rightfully so.

The issue of whether to pursue a particular goal or not is a very important one. If you are going to invest your time and energy in something, it should be right for you. It should be a fit. And that's the tricky part. What's a fit for you is not always obvious. It's also not obvious to everyone that there is such a thing as a right or wrong fit. Some feel, for example, that being a doctor is a good profession for anyone, without considering a person's talents or interests. This mistaken assumption, that anyone can or should be able to do anything and be happy, has caused a lot of people a lot of suffering.

How do you know if a goal is right for you? On what basis do you choose your goals? What or who chooses your goals? These are such important questions, because the answers determine the quality of your life and the extent of your happiness.

What makes you happy is actually a very good measure for what goals are a fit for you. You are meant to be happy, and the way you can be happy is to do what makes you happy *right now*. This may sound obvious, but many do things that do not fit for them in exchange for a *promise* of happiness in the future. However, if you always do what makes you happy, then you will always be happy!

It is your destiny to be happy—to follow your happiness. This is how the greater will guides life. The small will uses a stick—unhappiness in exchange for a promise of future happiness—while the greater will uses a carrot.

The issue of your happiness is not self-indulgent. Happiness is not just a personal goal but divine will—what the Father also wants for you. It is with happiness, or joy, that Life points you Homeward. And a happy person is kinder and serves life better than an unhappy one.

If you do not make conscious choices about your life, your conditioning will choose for you. This is not necessarily a problem with unimportant or short-range choices. However, if you are living mostly according to your conditioning, that is bound to feel dry, lifeless, lock-step, possibly even robotic or dead. If you feel this way, you can be sure that the ego has chosen your goals for you.

Life is so benevolent that it shows you when you are not aligned with it by causing something to feel off. You feel unmotivated and unhappy, lackluster or depressed. These feelings are a sign that you are following your conditioning. If you keep going in the ego's direction, these feelings will not go away. To feel differently, something will have to change.

For most people, this moment of truth is very difficult. "Now what? What will happen to me if I make a change?" The ego is afraid. Whenever you threaten to move away from the ego's control, it uses fear to reel you back in: "It's dangerous! You'll fail!"

The ego draws from your conditioning to try to convince you that you are wrong to contemplate some other possibility: "Remember when your uncle did that and failed. You've never been able to follow through on anything. You aren't smart enough. You're too old."

The ego uses fear, which it has been entrusted with to help you survive, to keep you under its control. The computer has taken over and will not be usurped! This might be humorous if the ego's fears were not so convincing—if fear did not seem so real and true. But convincing it is. Extremely so. Fear is the most powerful tool the ego has for keeping the illusion of the false self and its power intact.

The ego will come up with all sorts of ideas about what you should do next if you do decide that change is called for. However, those ideas will not get you out of the fix of living according to your conditioning, because those ideas are more of the same.

Whatever the thoughts in your mind are, they do not have the answer to how to live this life you have been given. Only the Life within you has the answer to how *it* wants to live through you. An answer to your dilemma exists, but it will not be found in your thoughts, only in your joy, which is the whisper of the greater will.

Everyone is familiar with the greater will—divine will—because it has been determining many of your choices despite the all-pervasive small will. Divine will works alongside the small will, offering alternatives and often acting in support of the small will.

The small will and divine will are not always at odds. In fact, divine will often bows to the small will, as it honors and celebrates many of the choices your humanness makes. Divine will, after all, created you as the human being that you are, and it created the ego and all the other programming to do exactly what it does.

The problem is that the small will sometimes overshadows divine will to the extent that life takes an unsatisfying direction. When people lose touch with their deeper guidance and only trust the mind, they are bound to make choices that leave them suffering and unhappy. When that happens, the solution is to realign with happiness by doing what you love and by letting joy move you moment by moment.

Living is an art! In order to stay on the road to happiness, peace, and love, it takes fine tuning of the art of listening to what is true for you in each moment. Fortunately, you can never permanently lose your way. The chapters to come have more to say about discovering and following what is true for you. But first, it is important to understand the specific programming that comprises the software.

Chapter 4

The Software

The software is a mix of useful, neutral, and not useful or harmful programming. One of the challenges with the software, besides some of it being outdated and limiting, is that sometimes the beneficial programming, such as that related to survival, is misapplied to situations outside of what it was designed for, with a negative result.

Fear is the best example of this. When one's physical safety is being immediately threatened, fear is useful. However, fear is not useful when a threat is not immediate but merely imagined. Most fear in modern society is of the imagined kind and has no practical purpose, although it is difficult to convince a person's body of that!

The more frequently a fear is imagined, the more believable it seems. And the more a fear is believed, the more often it will arise in the mind. The more often it arises, the stronger its effects in the body will be. And the stronger its effects, the more believable the fear will be. And so it goes. Human beings have learned to produce full-blown emotions simply by thinking. How creative!

For this to be possible, an advancement in brain development was necessary, which resulted in the imagination. What a boon imagination has been to the human race—and what immense suffering it has caused! This suffering is the very thing stimulating the next step in evolution, which is to move beyond this tendency to use the imagination negatively.

As human beings have evolved, so has their ability to think and imagine. And as the mind has become stronger, some of the more primitive aspects of the mind have too. Human beings are in the process of learning to cope with and weed out the useless and negative features of the mind and to use the mind more wisely. People are more aware than ever before of the power of beliefs and imagination on well-being and the experience of reality, and they are learning to master the mind so that fear and other emotions don't overwhelm or distort their experience.

Another useful but often misapplied aspect of the software is the mind's ability to come up with every possible thing that can go wrong. Being aware of negative possibilities can be helpful. However, if you let the computer-mind make choices for you based solely on problems you *might* encounter, you may never get out of bed.

The mind's tendency to focus on potential problems leaves people scared, joyless, and immobilized. Such cautionary warnings were never meant to overrun or hijack people's decisions. The computer-mind may provide some useful information, but information is just information, and it was never meant to run people's lives. For decisions that affect your life, you need wisdom, not just information. Fortunately, something very wise *is* running your life as long as you don't let the mind's fear and distrust of life override this wisdom.

Another aspect of the software that is often misapplied is the mind's ability to make comparisons and find fault. When you see two apples, the mind instantly assesses them and determines which apple is better. Or when the brain scans familiar territory, it instantly notices something new or out of place. The brain's ability to notice details, compare, contrast, and discriminate is immeasurably useful in this modern world, as it was when humans lived in the savannah or jungle and had to be on the lookout for predators.

In relationships, however, where love and cooperation are essential, this ability to notice flaws, compare, and judge does more to undermine survival and well-being than it does to help. The same could be said for your relationship with yourself: Judging and comparing yourself with others is not a winning strategy. Doing this doesn't further your survival or happiness but only interferes with fulfilling your potential and being at peace.

Some programming is not useful under any circumstances and can even be harmful. Most of the programming in this category consists of ideas and beliefs that are false, especially about yourself: "I'm not lovable. I'm not smart. I can't do that because.... I will never be...." Such ideas are never useful or helpful because they are a lie. They are a lie, because they are not the whole story.

Much of this type of programming is acquired in childhood, although the media and other sources continue to input lies and other limiting beliefs into the computer-mind throughout life. A child is told or taught something, and he or she believes it without questioning it, because a child doesn't have the intellectual or emotional resources to challenge the adults whom he or she is dependent on.

This information goes into the child's computer-mind, which repeats these messages mentally throughout life regardless of whether or not they are true. Those messages and judgments become the person's sense of self—the *you* that you come to see yourself as—which ultimately shapes reality and the person's experience of reality.

Just because a thought appears in your mind doesn't mean it is useful or even true. Everybody's mind is full of unquestioned falsehoods, which create unpleasant feelings and unnecessary limitation. If only people could see how untrustworthy their thoughts are, especially the ones about themselves, which is the majority of them! But the programming seems true, and so it goes unquestioned. The false self is built on such falsehoods and limiting ideas.

The faulty programming and the false self's power endure because most people do not question their thoughts and beliefs. But that's changing. The greater the number of people who question their mind, the easier it will be for others to question theirs. The result will be a revolution of consciousness. This revolution has begun, and the shift in consciousness will eventually transform the world you live in.

The software oversteps its bounds when it spills into thoughts. When programming turns into thoughts, the false self is created. The ego provides a *sense* of self, but when the ego begins talking to you and taking on the persona of being a self, that's where the trouble—the suffering—begins. It's as if you created a robot to help you with your chores, but instead it has taken over your identity and pretends to be you.

As long as the software stays in the background, operating the machinery of the body-mind, the software is not a problem. But when it takes on a voice, an identity, opinions, judgments, beliefs, desires, and fears, which pretend to be yours, then the programming becomes a problem. The reason this is a problem is that the false self is not you and is not wise, and yet it is believed to be you and given the power to be you—by you!

All is not lost, of course, because you are what is able to see this ruse and regain your power of choice—if you choose. The challenge is that this choice has to be made again and again—in every moment—because the false self doesn't disappear just because you have seen the truth about it. What it is up to has to be seen repeatedly, perhaps for years, until its position is so weakened that it is no longer experienced as real.

Once you have seen through the illusion of the false self thoroughly enough, it can no longer fool you, at least not for long. The false self may still exist, but it has been dethroned. It is a shadow of its former self and, like a shadow, is seen to have no substance.

Seeing through the illusion of the false self this completely is called *awakening*. You wake up out of the trance cast by the false self into the reality of your true being, the being that is awake and aware here and now and has been living through your body-mind and experiencing the false self for as long as you can remember.

What awakens is the *you* that consciously chooses, the *you* that is no longer overshadowed by the programming. This *you* may choose to follow some conditioned idea or belief or something else: an intuition, an urge, an impulse, a realization, an inspiration, a sense that says, "Go this way!"

What's different from before is that there is an experience of choice, of free will, and an acknowledgment of the responsibility that comes with that. You no longer blame circumstances or others for how you feel or what you experience, because you realize you are the creator of your inner experience and, to some extent, your outer experience. You create your feelings, you choose to respond to your conditioning or not, you choose the desires you go after, you choose what you give your attention to, and you choose your conclusions and beliefs. You are responsible for how you are in your life and, consequently, for your experience of life.

Another very important aspect of your software is the programming that is responsible for your personality. The choices you make, whether you are awake to the truth about the false self or not, tend to be shaped by this software to some extent. In creating a unique personality, this software highlights certain drives and desires, making certain choices and directions more likely.

Without this programming, human beings would be like clones of each other but, instead, everyone is unique. This uniqueness is part of the Creator's plan, since what would be the point of duplicating one's creations if their purpose is to provide the Creator with a one-of-a-kind experience and perspective?

To accomplish this uniqueness, each person receives programming that creates drives to move in particular directions and tendencies to behave in particular ways. For instance, some people are introverted and some are extroverted, some are playful and some are serious, some are adventuresome and some are cautious, some are leaders and some are followers, some are independent and some live for relationship. The list goes on. This programming is also responsible for particular interests and talents and for one's psychological issues.

Furthermore, as moving parts that belong to a greater Whole, every person has a pre-ascribed role and purpose within the Whole, which is also part of the software. This role and purpose are very generally described and guided by the software through specific drives, with a lot of room for free will to sketch out the details of how this role and purpose will be carried out.

These various aspects of the software define the character you are playing within the Whole, imprinting you with particular traits, desires, drives, attitudes, interests, and talents. The programming responsible for the personality creates a blueprint for the character you are playing and predispositions to behave in certain ways. But like all programming, it can be ignored or overridden by choosing to go against it and behave differently.

This programming doesn't change over the course of a lifetime, but how you express your personality and talents is very likely to evolve as you mature and learn better ways of using the personality, or vehicle, you have been given.

As in a play, everyone is given a character to play. But unlike a play, the script is not written, although each character's responses are somewhat predictable, since most adhere to their programming. Each character has free will and is free to choose how he or she responds to life, but the characters do not necessarily exercise that free will.

The character that you are playing can be ruled by the small will or the greater will. Most people's lives are ruled by some of both, alternating and to different degrees. But, as in a play, that character remains that character, regardless of what is driving or ruling it. Which will—the small will or the greater will—rules your character will deeply affect your character's experience of life and the life your character creates.

When the ego is what mostly rules the character, then egoic desires, fears, and a sense of lack motivate one's actions. The sense of lack the character feels will try to be filled by that character in a way that fits for it. For instance, if that character is relationship-oriented, it is likely to try to fill the ego's sense of lack through relationship.

A character that is driven by the ego may or may not fulfill its potentials, depending on how much the character allows the ego's fears and other conditioning to limit it. The ego is apt to steer that character in some unsatisfying directions that do not fit it, although that character might find its way to something more satisfying.

On the other hand, when the greater will is what primarily rules, then that character will be responsive to deeper, more meaningful desires and drives, which will result in the character being happy and fulfilling its destiny, or Thy will. That character is likely to achieve its potentials and purpose fairly easily, because it won't let the fears and limitations of the false self interfere. A character that is driven by the greater will is also more likely to attract the support of others in whatever it does because of its positive state of mind or state of no-mind.

Until you realize the power you have to choose your responses and determine your internal state, the character you are playing will be ruled by the ego's desires, fears, and sense of lack, and these will shape your choices and experience of reality. Your character will be involved in drama after drama, as Life attempts to wrestle the character from the grip of the illusion of the false self. The character will be at the mercy of the full range of human emotions, struggle with relationships, and have only brief moments of happiness.

This same character will have a very different experience of life once the character begins to exercise more free will. The gift of free will allows the character to become free of the suffering and drama caused by believing one's thoughts. In choosing not to believe the thoughts that run through the mind, the character is free to experience life without the pain and difficulties caused by egoic desires, judgments, worries, doubts, fears, and other negative thoughts and emotions. The character is free to simply enjoy life as it is, free of the false self's desires and ideas of what life should or should not be and free of the ego's need to control life. The life that lies outside the kingdom of the false self is a very bright one indeed.

You are meant to be the character you are playing! And you are meant to be happy as this character. The ego will play this character in a way that will make you feel unhappy with yourself. You will never feel good enough, be good enough, or have enough. But once the ego is returned to its rightful place, as software running in the background, you can fully enjoy yourself as this character, while knowing that you are much more than this.

When the ego is in control, the character feels like who you are and the character's shortcomings and imperfections seem unacceptable. They are a source of pain and a problem to be fixed. But when you know who you *really* are, the character can be the imperfect character that it is. It is lovable in its imperfection and for its uniqueness.

Who you really are is the *you* that loves the character you are playing and every other character. It sees through every character's costume to the universal life force that enlivens each. This *you* is in love with life just as it is. What a miracle life is! And what a miracle every character is!

CHAPTER 5

The Chooser

What awakens from the illusion of the false self is the true self, although the true self was never asleep. This is a paradox and where words fall short. Something has always been awake and has never slept—Consciousness, your true nature. And yet the human drama is of one who has fallen asleep to the truth and then awakens to it. Both are true and both have been happening simultaneously.

I will refer to the self that awakens or is awakening as *the chooser*, because it is capable of choosing more consciously than before. However, all along, this chooser was choosing at least some of the time. What changes after the illusion of the false self is thoroughly seen through is that you experience yourself as the chooser instead of the false self. It is an experience of being outside the mind and noticing your thoughts rather than feeling like you are the one thinking your thoughts. Awakening is a waking up out of the mind.

This is a very important step along the way to enlightenment and makes happiness and peace much more accessible. And yet, conditioning remains that needs to be seen through, choices have to be made, and there is a new way of being in the world to get used to. If you are no longer the false self and, for the most part, no longer being driven by its desires and fears, then how *do* you move in the world? What moves you?

Many people experience a dropping away of motivation at this stage, but what actually drops away are the ego's goals and the drive to achieve them, not motivation itself. When the ego's goals no longer seem attractive, motivation may seem to have disappeared, but it is still there. It just doesn't look or feel like motivation looked and felt before.

After awakening, often the only motivation is to just *be*. Just being may seem like doing nothing and may seem absent of motivation, since that's how the ego would view it, but just being is actually doing something. It's just not something the ego would choose to do.

The being that you are loves to just be and just experience whatever it is experiencing. It is fascinated by things the ego wouldn't consider interesting at all. The being that you are finds everything wondrous and delightful. It is easily pleased and content. To be happy, your being doesn't need the flash, glamour, activity, and excitement that the ego needs. Just being and experiencing are enough.

Once adjustments to this new state of greater awakeness have been made, you will be drawn again to being more active in the world, but your motivation will come from something other than the small will. It will come from a greater will, which moves you, not with thoughts, but in other ways.

Just because the ego has lost control and fallen into the background doesn't mean the egoic commentary in your head ceases, however. The programming is still there, and the false self still exists and has some power to hook you back into believing it. But when you do get hooked, the experience of identification is different than before, because now you are more aware.

The chooser obviously doesn't choose to identify with conditioning—that just happens. As conditioning surfaces from the unconscious mind, it commands attention for a while and may even produce feelings. But, unlike before awakening, the chooser is too awake to not notice that identification. And once the chooser becomes aware of identification, the chooser can choose to do something about it.

Before, when your will was identical with the small will, the will was used to choose between conflicting desires or beliefs, not to free yourself from conditioning altogether. The choice was between being thin or eating a piece of cake, for example, which are conflicting egoic desires. Now the choice is between staying identified with the ego, or conditioning, or not staying identified with it.

The chooser wants something quite outside what the small will wants. In fact, the chooser wants something the small will doesn't want at all. The chooser wants freedom from the suffering caused by the incessant desires of the small will. It wants freedom to simply enjoy life just as it is, freedom from the ego's dissatisfaction and sense that something is missing or not right and needs changing.

This deep desire for freedom comes from beyond the ego and drives human evolution forward. This desire and the will that supports it are very different from the ego's desires and will. The ego's desires, which fuel the small will, are based on conditioned ideas and the belief that something essential to happiness is lacking, which is not true.

The false self is a self that feels lacking. It is trying to get or become something that it believes is necessary for happiness. The desires that fuel the small will are based on false presumptions. Nothing is actually lacking; only the *belief* that something is lacking makes it seem so. Attaining the ego's desires will never satisfy that sense of lack anyway, because the ego will continue to manufacture that sense of lack regardless of what is attained.

On the other hand, the greater will, which the chooser draws upon, is based on deeper desires and drives that, although very real and true, are more subtle and less tangible than the desires, feelings, and drives of the ego. As a result, the greater will cannot be understood by the mind and is therefore not felt to be real by the mind. So, these deeper desires are often overlooked or disregarded by the mind.

What powers the greater will is not lack but the desire to live in joy, peace, and love, which is the drive for enlightenment. This drive is at the heart of life and at the heart of everyone. Joy, peace, and love are what everyone is seeking. How wonderful it is that these are what propel life and what evolution ultimately delivers!

How does the greater will bring about joy, peace, and love? It does this by inspiring you to move in ways that create more joy, peace, and love. Just as the small will creates conflict, stress, and suffering by moving you in ways that create conflict, stress, and suffering, the greater will moves you in ways that create joy, peace, and love. You know whether you are aligned with the small will or the greater will by the results.

What you choose is what you get. When you do not realize *that* you are choosing or *what* you are choosing, you get what the ego wants and what it creates, because the programming will rule. However, when you are conscious of choosing and conscious of what you are choosing, you naturally choose what brings joy, peace, and love. When the ego is no longer choosing, all that's left is what chooses to move in a way that produces joy, love, and peace rather than suffering. The choice is made for you by your true nature, by the greater will. Then Thy will, will be done.

Before Thy will is what determines your every choice, there is an in-between stage in which you experience yourself as having to choose between the small will and the greater will and when the programming still chooses at times. Nevertheless, something very important has shifted since you were at the mercy of your programming: Now you are aware of when you have become identified. You are aware of when you have let the programming choose.

This may not seem like a big shift, since you still suffer at times from getting hooked by the old programming, but this is vastly different from being at the mercy of your conditioning, when your free will was subsumed by the small will. The difference is that now you are in a position of being able to choose to stay awake or fall back to sleep. There is no wrong choice, as it is perfectly acceptable to fall back to sleep—to re-identify with your programming—if you choose. Life is so benevolent that it allows you a choice.

Now that you know yourself as the chooser, it's much more difficult to ignore or go against the truth you have seen. It is quite painful to go back to sleep once you have experienced what it is like to be awake. The knowledge of what this is like inspires you to continue to choose to stay awake.

And so, just as you might briefly fall asleep after you first awaken in the morning, you might fall asleep from time to time before you more fully awaken. But one thing is certain: You will fully awaken at some point, because it is time—you have already seen the light of day. Some people just have a longer period of drowsiness than others.

Some conditioned beliefs have staying power and still feel very true even after awakening, even though you know they aren't true. Something deep within you still believes that belief, and so this misunderstanding, this mistaken belief, will have to be addressed through some kind of healing.

The most difficult conditioning to overcome is that which is formed in early childhood and in other lifetimes. Many of these issues will need some kind of guide, such as a therapist or healer, to assist you in working through them, while less emotionally charged beliefs can probably be worked through on your own by bringing your loving and compassionate awareness to them and investigating them until they relax their hold. Much has already been written about how to do this healing work by this author and others, so I will not be much more explicit here. The point is, as long as you have unhealed conditioning, which is true of nearly everyone, it will pull you into identification with the false self to some extent.

Fortunately, once you know that you are not the false self, healing conditioning is much easier to do, because you are more able to be aware of the false self's mistaken beliefs and negative feelings, accept them, and bring compassion to them. What heals conditioning are these three qualities of attention: awareness, acceptance, and compassion.

Since identifying with conditioning can still happen without any conscious choice on your part even after awakening, your only choice is what you do once you find yourself hooked by a mistaken belief or negative feeling. If you don't consciously choose to do something when you first get hooked, then the old programs will probably take over, and you will find yourself even more deeply identified.

How you relate to conditioning once you get hooked will either help it to dissolve or reinforce it. If you react to or act out a feeling or a thought, such as a story or judgment, the way you used to, then that thought or feeling will be reinforced and is guaranteed to return, perhaps even stronger. On the other hand, if you are able to realize that you are hooked, then you can choose to relate to that thought or feeling differently than you have in the past.

Here's how to relate to a story or some other thought or feeling that you are identified with: First, simply notice what you are experiencing. What is the experience of the story or feeling like in your body, both physically and energetically? Where do you feel it? What does it feel like? Tight? Dark? Hollow? Heavy? Sharp? Cool? Hot? Let the sensations that are there be there and stay with them for a few moments. Let yourself feel them fully without any mental commentary.

Next, give the complex of sensations a name, address it, befriend it, and get to know it: "Welcome, sadness (or pain, tightness, smallness, shame, fear, or whatever). There is room for you here. Why have you come? And what have you to say?" Then listen to the feeling or story with your whole being. Don't try to analyze it or figure it out with your mind. Just listen and see if you can discover from the feeling or story what thoughts or beliefs lie beneath it. An intuition might arise about this. If not, just continue to allow the sensations to be present.

Next, notice what else is present besides the feeling or story. Is acceptance here? Love? Compassion? Judgment? Desire? Beauty? Other sensations? Other feelings? Gratitude? Peace? So many things can be present in one moment. Notice everything and let everything be as it is.

Allow and drink in the rich composite of experience that is the present moment. Doing this helps put the story or feeling in perspective. The story or feeling is just one of so many things present in the moment, and you are so much more than any of those things.

You are the marvelous, gracious Presence that is experiencing it all and in love with it all. In acknowledging and accepting everything that is present in a particular moment in this way, you naturally move into alignment with your loving nature, which is at peace with life just as it is.

Making such choices moves you from identification and suffering to disidentification and freedom from suffering. Although this process may need to be repeated many times and may take some time, these are the kinds of choices that will help you heal your conditioning rather than be victimized by it.

There is one other choice you can make when you are caught in conditioning, especially when you are suffering and struggling with false beliefs and difficult feelings: Pray! Every prayer for assistance is heard and answered. Do not hesitate to call for help from me and from others who exist to serve you. Never doubt that you are loved and cared for in every moment of your life. You are never alone, and help is always available.

But you must choose to ask! We do not interfere with your free will by imposing help that is not asked for. We respect your choice to hold yourself apart from us and rejoice when you turn to us for assistance. Know this and be at peace!

Chapter 6

Nothing to Choose

Choosing presupposes two or more things to choose from. When there are not two or more choices, then there is nothing to choose. In other words, when there is only one viable choice, what is there to choose? This one choice is often called a *choiceless choice.* The choiceless choice is what God wants or, you could say, what Life wants.

When you experience yourself as the chooser, you experience the possibility of two choices in any moment: what the small will would choose or what the greater will, or Life, *is* choosing. But when the small will is no longer a player, that is, when the ego has lost its power, then all that is left is the greater will.

When only the greater will remains, then that is not experienced so much as will but as just what is unfolding naturally in the moment. This sweet and innocent unfolding of life is a reflection of the greater will.

The sense of there being nothing to choose is often described as going with the flow of life. Since life is constantly on the move, going with the flow means going in the direction that life is already moving. This flow or direction is also called the Tao. When the small will wants to go in some other direction than the flow, that desire creates the experience of needing to choose between that direction or the flow.

The experience of being so in the flow that there is no longer a need to choose is also described as there being no one to choose: The chooser has disappeared because there is nothing to choose between. But the chooser doesn't completely disappear until the small will drops away and ceases to have any power. Until then, the experience of having to choose and the sense of there being a chooser remains.

When the false self and its will are no longer experienced as who you are and what you want, and this is realized deeply and thoroughly, you are left with an experience of *no self*: no one to choose. In the absence of a self, all there is, is Consciousness, living and breathing as life itself, one united and indivisible being—God—manifesting as you and everything else. This is not like any self you have ever experienced before!

Although the basic software still runs the body-mind as needed, someone who is experiencing no self doesn't refer to conditioning for how to behave or move. He or she is moved by the only will that is left: by Life. That person takes his or her cue from life as life is showing up moment to moment, and moves accordingly.

Living this way may sound impossible and impractical, but I can assure you that this is how you are meant to live and how all of humanity will live in the future. The future of the human race is an enlightened humanity. Few live this way now, but more and more will be living like this before long, because it is time for humanity to make a leap forward in its evolution. Many of you are the harbingers of this great shift in consciousness.

Will underlies all of creation, which itself is an act of will. Life is directed by divine intention, divine will. There is method to this miraculous madness! If what is behind life is anything, it is intelligent. This must be apparent to you: An incomprehensible Intelligence is at the helm, and it is steered by will and intention.

Intention for what? How can this even be known? We can make certain assumptions about this Intelligence based on what divine will has already accomplished through its creations. This Intelligence must have an intention to experience, learn, and evolve, since that is obviously going on. It must also have an intention to create, since that is also going on. And it must have an intention to be challenged, since that, too, is woven into the fabric of life.

These are all things that God could not experience without willing creation into existence and designing it specifically to provide these things. With creation comes the potential to experience, learn, evolve, create, and be challenged. None of this could have been experienced before creation existed.

The great sages of India call this act of divine creation *lila*, which means play. Creation is how God takes on various roles and guises, explores an array of choices and desires, challenges Himself/Herself, and evolves. God loves doing all these things, just as you do. As above, so below. You are God playing at being a human being.

Life is being intelligently directed by divine will. The ego doesn't share this perspective, however, but quite the opposite one. The ego feels tossed to and fro by a dangerous and likely meaningless universe, forever at the mercy of misfortune and unjust fate.

The ego's perspective is most certainly a recipe for suffering! If you believe this about life, you will feel the way your ego does: victimized, frightened, angry, inadequate, vulnerable, and justified in looking out for #1.

The ego's beliefs and feelings invariably lead to harmful, selfish, and hurtful actions, which create the painful, dog-eat-dog reality that the ego assumes reality to be. The ego's belief that this is a misbegotten world is reinforced, and the cycle continues: Perception creates reality or, at the very least, one's experience of reality.

Life is so benevolent that it allows human beings to have whatever experiences they choose to create, even painful ones. Although God designed life to have challenges, including the challenge of having an ego, God does not create painful experiences. People create pain out of the challenges they are given by their attitude toward them, which is shaped by the stories they tell themselves. And God allows people to do that.

Fortunately, the ego's perceptions of reality are not the truth, which people are bound to discover, thanks to the gift of suffering. With every challenge, you are asked to rise above and move beyond the distorted perceptions of your software, which create a painful and conflict-ridden experience of reality. The software is corrupt!

Discovering this is the first step in overcoming the difficulties and suffering caused by believing the lies fabricated by the software. Dispelling these illusions is no small task. This is where inquiry comes in.

Inquiry is a method that uses the mind—your intelligence—to see through the illusions and falsehoods cast by the aspect of the mind that has taken on an identity as *you*. This aspect of the mind is often called the *egoic mind*, because it is essentially an expression of the ego and your conditioning, of your software.

I have been referring to the egoic mind as the thoughts that run through your mind, or the false self. The egoic mind could also be described as the software that has taken on a voice and an identity and speaks to you in your own mind as if it is you or an authority figure, a guide, a friend, a mentor, a parent, a judge, or some other persona.

Through inquiry, you probe, "Who is it that has this judgment, belief, opinion, feeling, desire, hope, dream, memory, or story? Who is this *I*?" You sit with this question and take some time to look for the *I*. When you look for the thinker of a thought, you cannot find it. The self that seems to be you doesn't exist!

That sense of *you* is created by a string of thoughts, all of which can be seen to have arisen on their own, unbidden and not chosen by you. The self that seems like you is literally generated by thoughts that come out of nowhere. The computer-mind spits out thoughts, you feel like they are yours, and so you become caught in the illusion of the false self.

Another very basic but very important inquiry is simply asking if a thought is true. All this requires is turning your ability to objectively observe, which is an aspect of your intelligence and also of Intelligence, onto your egoic mind. When you do this, you discover quite quickly that most of the thoughts that run through your mind are not true or are true only some of the time.

Although it is easy enough to discover the truth about your thoughts, you have to be willing to look. Inquiry is making the choice to look and see what is true rather than hide your head in the sand and carry on as usual. Besides willingness, or will, looking in this way takes courage and a deep curiosity about the truth, not only about a specific thought, but also about thoughts in general. Is this mass of computer programming really what you want to base your life and well-being on?

The will to look deeply into what is true and the courage and curiosity to do this doesn't come from the ego but from who you are. And it comes when it is time to awaken. There is no mistake in not having investigated your thoughts sooner. Everything unfolds in its own time. The will to look and investigate comes when a person is ready to awaken from the illusion of being a suffering self.

After you experience through inquiry that the self that you thought you were doesn't exist except as thoughts, another inquiry you can do, which will lead to an experience of your true self, is: "Who is it that is aware of this judgment, belief, opinion, feeling, desire, hope, dream, memory, or story?" That question drops you immediately into the experience of yourself as Awareness. What you really are is not the thinker of the thoughts but what is *aware* of the thoughts. That aware Presence is who you really are.

I mention inquiry because it is key in unraveling the illusion around who you are. This type of inquiry is essential before you can begin to see reality from a clear, true perspective, one not muddied by the ego's mistaken assumptions and misperceptions.

Until you experience your true self for yourself, what I or others say about who you really are will remain theoretical and not that believable. Because you cannot believe the truth and what the ego believes simultaneously, since these perspectives are mutually exclusive, you have to see through the ego's lies to some extent before you can experience the truth. Inquiry helps you do that.

Letting go of the ego's perceptions is not so easy. It can be scary. Inquiry leads to a radical paradigm shift, and people do not easily choose to shake up their beliefs by asking such deep questions. Only those who are ready for this leap in consciousness will venture to do inquiry. The ego has its way of keeping people in its grip, and denial and fear are its strongest allies.

So, I can tell you that life is good and trustworthy and that it is unfolding perfectly, but will you believe this? Will this be enough for you to *know* this? Unfortunately, I cannot make you feel and know this truth just by saying it. You must be willing to do these inquiries and make this leap of faith yourself.

This leap of faith is essentially a choice, a very important one. Once you choose to believe a new, truer, and more positive version of life, then that will become your experience of reality. Beliefs are that powerful!

If you do not already have beliefs that create a positive reality, one free of suffering, then you must choose to believe new beliefs. At a certain point, that is the only choice left, because you see that the only other option is to go back to suffering. This point is like standing on a precipice, with your old life behind you and a new one waiting for you—if only you step off the cliff.

Try on the beliefs presented here and see how they feel. Let your heart be your guide: Do these beliefs bring more happiness, harmony, peace, prosperity, and love into your life or not? Are the beliefs you have now working for you? Do they bring you what you really want? If not, you have nothing to lose in discarding them.

Once you choose to believe that life is good and trustworthy, you drop into the flow and the chooser disappears, because there is no longer any inner conflict. This is the last choice: You choose to believe the truth about life. Then you don't have to choose again, because you *become* the Truth—the Light. When your beliefs are aligned with the Truth, they are like a key that unlocks the great beauty of your Being, and the door to a new world opens for you.

Finally, you are no longer at odds with yourself. There is only one direction to move in. When you choose to believe the truth about life, all other choices drop away, and you find yourself in harmony with all of life. All that is left is what is unfolding in this moment, and that is enough—more than enough. It is heaven on earth.

Chapter 7

The Truth

I will tell you the truth about life. The truth is actually very simple: *Life is perfect just as it is.* This includes you! You are perfect just as you are and so is everyone else. *There is no problem to fix*, although fixing and improvements naturally happen. *There is nothing that needs to be different*, although everything is in the process of changing and becoming different. *There is nothing lacking* within you or in any moment, although everything is, paradoxically, evolving and becoming more of what it already is. *You are eternal*, although your body is not. *You are Divine Consciousness*, although you are not always aware of that. *Love and goodness are your true nature*, although this is not always your experience.

These truths are immutable. They might not appear to be true at times, but that is an illusion. When the sky is covered over with clouds, it seems to have disappeared, but the sky is always there and always blue behind the clouds. The sky's nature and appearance never change; only the clouds prevent you from seeing it.

When the blue sky is not visible, you still trust that it exists, because you know the truth about the sky and the truth about the clouds. The same is true regarding the truth about life: Once you realize the Truth, you can draw upon that realization when the Truth is obscured by fear or a mistaken idea. You can remind yourself of the Truth, and that is often enough to regain perspective.

You can always be fooled again by the illusion cast by your thoughts, feelings, and desires, because you are human. There will always be ideas and feelings that seem very real, which can entangle you in their illusory reality. But once you know the Truth, you cannot be fooled in the same way or lost in the illusion for long, because you know that blue sky is behind those clouds and that, at some point, the clouds will part and the Truth will be clearly seen again.

The truth can actually be summed up in one sentence: *Everything is unfolding perfectly.* So, let us explore this great truth a little more fully.

First of all, notice what happens in your body when you take in this truth. The body melts into relaxation and gives a great sigh of relief, because if it is true that everything is unfolding perfectly, then all the striving to fix yourself and the struggling against life can stop. Finally, you can just *be*.

What it is that you get to be is your true self, which is in love with life—which *is* love and *is* life. When you stop trying to fix and change the way things are, you discover who you really are, and who you are is everything you have ever wanted to be.

The real truth, that everything is unfolding perfectly, is the exact opposite of the ego's truth! A definition of the ego might be the programming that causes you to see lack and imperfection everywhere and that compels you to try to fix, change, and improve things, including your experience. This programming also compels you to seek solace in pleasure and seek happiness in desire-fulfillment to cope with the stress and suffering caused by this endless improvement project.

This project to improve yourself and to fix and change things is an effort on the part of the ego to keep you safe. The ego is dedicated to being vigilant about all the ways you might improve yourself or your situation. That is its constant focus. Even in the absence of any real problems, the egoic mind can easily enumerate many things that, according to it, need fixing or improving: "Lose five pounds. Be nicer. Take longer walks. Read more books. Eat more fiber. Get enlightened. Fix your relationship with your mother. Get a relationship."

What is not always obvious about the ego's suggestions, however, is that many are things you have little control over, although the implication is that you do. For example, is it really in your power to get enlightened or to get a relationship or to fix your relationship with your mother? These are tall orders for the little ego to fill! It's best to leave such things up to something wiser and more powerful.

The implication that you can and should be able to make life be the way you would like it to be through your own efforts is a false assumption on the part of the ego, which is in denial about its own lack of control. The ego takes the fact that you do have some control in life to mean that you can and should have complete control, which of course is wishful thinking on the part of the ego.

As well-meaning as the ego's lists may seem, they make you feel inadequate, burdened, overwhelmed, and like a failure when you don't achieve everything on them. Such lists are a source of suffering more than they are helpful. But they do help the ego sustain the illusion that you are a self that is forever lacking, which gives the ego a reason for existing.

Most moments are filled with thoughts about what is missing or wrong and what you might do about it. The mind is in the habit of thinking such thoughts, and people are in the habit of taking the bait and agreeing with the mind that there are all these problems that need fixing. It's not that there are not real problems that need to be solved and things that need to be fixed, but the mind creates problems where there were none.

The mind comes up with problems and solutions, because the mind was designed to do this. In so doing, the ego is trying to be helpful and *is* helpful sometimes. However, the ego often tries to manage people's lives in ways that are not helpful and also not appropriate. It's not that there isn't some value in this aspect of the software, but for the mind's suggestions to become a way of life gives the software too much power—power that it was not designed to have.

When you are no longer in the ego's grip, all there is, is peace and the realization that everything is unfolding perfectly. But how will you discover this if you have been trained that not doing or not striving is equal to laziness, that such relaxed being and flowing with life is, in a sense, immoral, according to the ego's values? When the ego is god, then doing is god and not doing or just being is the opposite of god, the opposite of good. Just being becomes bad or is at least seen to have no value.

The illusion is set up very cleverly to maintain itself, and it is maintained by beliefs such as these: Doing is good and just being is bad. Because beliefs are what maintain the illusion, it makes sense that beliefs are what must be examined—and changed—to become free of the illusion.

Let's examine this idea of doing. Does "Everything is unfolding perfectly" mean that you don't have to do anything or that you won't do anything if you believe this? On some level, this is what the mind would argue, although if you examine this argument, it falls apart.

Of course you would still do things even if you believed that everything was unfolding perfectly. How could you not do things? It is impossible to do nothing. You would naturally do what you needed to do to survive, whether your mind told you what to do or not.

You do not need your egoic mind to tell you how to survive. The belief that you need it to survive is part of the illusion. The software working in the background takes care of basic survival without the egoic mind needing to manage your every move, and your own wise being does the rest. The egoic mind is the aspect of the computer-mind that pretends to be useful but isn't.

If you believed that everything was unfolding perfectly, you would discover that you are naturally motivated by something other than the push and sense of lack of the ego. Without the ego's motivation, the greater will—the flow—would move you, and always has to some extent.

When you are in the flow, just being moves naturally into doing when necessary and then back into just being when doing is no longer necessary. By just being, you are renewed, readied for, and informed of whatever arises next to be done. What that is, comes out of the flow, and just being makes it possible to be aware of that. When you are in the flow, you experience a natural cycling of being and doing that serves the flow.

Everything is unfolding perfectly means that whatever you do, even if it is motivated by the small will, is part of the perfect unfolding of the moment. Some would argue that some actions could not belong to the perfect unfolding. For example, could a crime be part of the perfect unfolding? The answer is yes, because the Perfection includes free will and allows for *any* possible choice you could make. That's why it's called *free* will. You are free to do anything.

Choosing whatever you choose is not a problem for the unfolding of life, because Life adjusts to and includes whatever you choose in the unfolding. By "adjusts," I mean that Life, the flow, responds accordingly, so Life's intent will continue to be fulfilled no matter what you choose. In this way, life is like a river: If a tree falls into the river, the river continues to flow in the same direction, but it adjusts its course slightly.

You see, you cannot change the flow of life dramatically. You can only cause it to make adjustments. You *affect* the flow, but you do not change the flow. You are not powerful enough to change it. The flow is proceeding in a particular direction, and it adjusts to your choices, but it is not changed by those choices.

All of the doing the ego engages in is like ripples in the river of Life, in this ever-unfolding Perfection. Like a child playing in the river, the child splashes, but the river is still the river, and it still moves in the direction it is moving in.

Your free will is not a match for the greater will. When the small will is not aligned with the greater will, the greater will always wins. Nevertheless, the greater will often allows the small will to get what it wants even when that desire is not aligned with the greater will, because the greater will intends for you to learn from your choices so that you will choose more wisely in the future.

For this reason, there are no wrong choices. All choices lead to greater wisdom, and what could be wrong with that? So, poor choices—ones that cause suffering—are part of the perfect unfolding of life. Such choices are an expected part of life and not a problem for the Perfection and do not mar it. When growth and evolution are part of the Perfection, then choices that lead to growth can only be perfect as well. The Perfection is such that it was designed to bring people Home to the realization of their true nature. Since all choices lead Home, no course that anyone might take can be off-course or wrong.

A corollary to the great truth that everything is unfolding perfectly is that, in any moment, *you are having exactly the right experience.* The small will and the greater will are co-creating your experience perfectly to bring you Home or accomplish some other intention or lesson. You cannot have a wrong experience!

Every experience accomplishes something, if not directly and immediately, then indirectly and at some later time.

Whatever is happening is meant to be happening. If what is happening is not the direct intention of divine will, then what is happening is the intention of the small will, either your small will or someone else's, and being allowed by divine will for some reason. It is being allowed because something needs to be learned by everyone involved. If you are involved in someone else's lesson, then it is also yours.

When you see your experiences as having been designed for you, then you can begin to realize the truth that everything is an opportunity for growth and for developing love, compassion, wisdom, strength, courage, and other virtues. Life is designed to stretch you, and it does that very well!

Not being able to understand why you are experiencing something doesn't mean you shouldn't be experiencing it. People often assume that because some event or experience doesn't make sense to them that they live in a capricious or even evil universe. But this is not the case.

The Intelligence behind life is neither capricious nor evil but quite the opposite. The intent of this Intelligence is always for evolution and movement toward greater love, peace, understanding, compassion, wisdom, and strength. There are no mistakes and no wrong experiences. *Everything you experience is taking you Home* and, in so doing, making you more loving and wise.

For example, if you are feeling a sense of drudgery, then that is the right experience. The sense of drudgery was created by something—some thought. If that is not the experience you want, if it doesn't give you peace and happiness, then find out how you created that experience and create a better one. You are meant to learn to create peace and happiness and to become more loving in life and more loving of life. With the incentive of suffering, everyone eventually succeeds in learning these things.

Even the experience of pain in your body is the right experience. Pain draws your attention to something that needs taking care of. It is part of the software that protects you. Or if there is nothing more you can do for the pain, then the pain is meant to be experienced just as it is.

Pain is an opportunity to discover the power of your thoughts and feelings to create added suffering, to add insult to injury, as they say. The more stories, worries, and fears you add to the pain, the worse the pain gets. When pain is stripped of such thoughts, it is just a sensation. It is reality showing up as a painful sensation, which is just part of having a body. This is not to deny the existence of terrible pain that sometimes must be endured, but when that is the case, endurance of that pain is what is meant to be, for whatever reason.

There are always reasons for experiencing whatever you are experiencing, but you often do not or cannot know what those reasons are. One of the challenges of being human is to have faith that there is always a reason for whatever you are experiencing. Every experience serves your evolution and the evolution of the Whole, and that is the reason, although there are almost always many reasons, many ways, that an experience serves. Faith in this can eliminate a lot of suffering.

"This shouldn't be happening!" screams the ego. But what if you really knew that whatever was happening *should* be happening? What if you met each moment with the realization that *this should be happening*? How different that would be. It would be a better experience, wouldn't it?

Just notice how much better it feels in your body to believe that something should be happening instead of that it shouldn't be happening. How it feels in the body is a clue to what the real truth is. The truth is whatever allows you to feel at peace with life.

You are having exactly the right experience also goes for your state of consciousness. Where you are in your spiritual evolution is exactly where you are meant to be. If you are not awake or enlightened right now, then you are not meant to be awake or enlightened right now. If you are struggling and contracted, then that is the right experience. And if you are at peace and expanded, then that is the right experience. Whatever you are experiencing is the right experience!

The ego would like to think it can control your state and your spiritual progress. But something much more mysterious is in control of this, and it is very wise and having exactly the experience it wants to have through you. You are co-creating with this mysterious will, but your choices have only so much impact on your spiritual unfoldment. One of the most important choices you can make is to choose to believe that the experience you are having is the right experience.

When you don't believe this, you are left with the opposite belief—that you shouldn't be having the experience you are having. This belief only leads to suffering and being at odds with life. So, why wouldn't you choose to believe that the experience you are having is the experience you should be having, even if you weren't sure? What is there to lose?

The Truth has to be taken on faith to some extent. But isn't that also true of the ego's truth? And yet people take the ego's perspective as true. Is the ego's truth that much more believable than the Truth? Is there actually more evidence for the ego's truth than for the Truth? Or is it just the programming that makes the ego's truth seem more believable?

The only way out of the mistaken perceptions and suffering caused by such powerful, yet untrue, programming is to question the programming and question it again and again, and then replace that faulty programming with truer programming. Your beliefs can be changed, although doing this is no small thing and not accomplished overnight.

Through repetition, the egoic mind has managed to convince you of many things that aren't true. By repeating the Truth to yourself, you can convince your mind of the Truth and erase your mind's previous beliefs. Those who try to manipulate people's beliefs, such as advertisers, do this all the time. They repeat their message again and again, because they know that messages heard repeatedly become true to the brain, whether they are true or not. If you hear something often enough, you begin to believe it. So, tell yourself the Truth again and again.

The truth is, you are having exactly the right experience for your growth or for some other reason. The only reason this doesn't seem so at times is that the ego wants life to be a certain way. When the ego's desires are not being met, it assumes that it isn't having the right experience: "How dare life be different than what I want! Something is wrong here." Usually the only thing wrong is one's thinking, and that is often the lesson.

Life does not exist to fulfill the ego's desires and dreams. Life is also not out to dash them. It's just that desires and dreams are not the measure for what is meant to be. The rightness or even justness of life cannot be measured by whether life is going according to the ego's desires or ideas about how it should go. The ego's desires and fantasies are in the realm of illusion, not reality. The purpose and intent of Life is much greater and more all-encompassing than people's desires and dreams.

So, how do you know what Life wants? Although you cannot know the will of the Divine, you can know how divine will is manifesting in your life by observing what it is giving you or allowing you to create and what it is not allowing you to have or create. Whatever that is, is what Life intends. Whatever Life gives or does not give, brings or does not bring, belongs to the perfect unfolding.

There is a divine design, and you are a participant in it. The Divine's intentions are being revealed in every moment. To discover what is meant to be, all you have to do is notice what is already happening. What is supposed to be is what already is! And who knows what will be next? You will discover that in the next moment.

Life is happening, and it is happening exactly as it is meant to be happening. What a relief! You are along for the ride, steering the boat a little with your tiny oar. God gives you the oar, but you do not control the river. You can do whatever you want, and nothing you do is ever judged as a problem. Nothing you do can put you out of God's heart, for you are God's beloved. You are loved more than you can ever imagine.

Are you willing to believe this? Are you willing to be humble enough to admit that you don't know how life should or shouldn't be or how your life should or shouldn't be? This is a good starting point. If you are at least able to admit that you might not know what is best for you and your life, then you have a better chance of seeing that something that you are assuming isn't good for you actually is. This humility will go a long way in easing any suffering.

Life is mysterious and works in mysterious ways. You cannot know or understand the workings of the vast Intelligence behind life. But know that the Intelligence is unfolding life perfectly regardless of how it may look. Know this, believe this, and bring this understanding to each moment, and your life will be transformed. Once the Truth is believed, life is never the same.

Chapter 8

Living the Truth

A belief in the Truth is like a boat that carries you to the Truth. Once you are in the Truth, you no longer need the belief because you *know* the Truth. But as long as you are involved in beliefs—the ego's beliefs—then a belief about the Truth is the boat that can take you to another state of consciousness.

By choosing to believe the Truth, you drop into the Truth, the truth about life. Just as believing the ego's truth made the ego's reality real, believing the Truth makes reality *as it actually is* real. All along, reality was what it is, but reality seemed so much harsher when you believed the ego's beliefs about it and trusted what the mind said.

Beliefs are all that create the illusion—nothing more. Like smoke, beliefs have no substance, and yet they create a seemingly real and true experience of life, until you see otherwise. Then you realize you were mistaken—fooled.

Usually being fooled doesn't feel good, and so you have defenses, such as denial and hiding your head in the sand, to prevent you from feeling foolish. Such defenses maintain the illusion and make it harder to discover the truth about life.

When people are attached to their beliefs, the truth is not as important to them as not feeling fooled and foolish. They don't want to know the truth as much as they don't want to discover that they have been fooled, which is very humbling. The ego has quite a lot of ways of keeping people fooled for a very long time.

Wanting to know the truth is the turning point. This desire arises from your true nature when it is time to awaken. It is God's calling card. You can only put off answering the call so long before you *must* know the truth, even if it means discovering that you have been fooled. To know the Truth, you have to be willing to feel like a fool! You have to be willing to be humbled—and then you are raised.

Although you have to be *willing* to be humbled to discover the truth, discovering the truth is not actually humbling or upsetting, as it would seem to the ego, because the ego is not in the picture anymore. The dissolving of the illusion is also the dissolving of the ego. Instead of feeling bad, discovering the truth feels more like waking up from a bad dream: You are just happy that what you thought was true isn't.

When you awaken, the truth you discover is that you are naturally loving, peaceful, content, and happy and that anytime you didn't feel or behave that way, it was only because you believed a lie. Now, because you are no longer fooled by the ego's lies, the whole nightmare created by them has disappeared into thin air along with the dissatisfied, unpleasant, struggling, not-good-enough self.

When you were dreaming, you felt frightened, confused, and at the mercy of whatever was going on. When you are awake to life as it actually is, you feel the opposite: safe, relaxed, at peace, content, and clear. These are two very different states of consciousness. One was manufactured by your beliefs, and the other is your natural state, which has always been available to you, although often clouded over by the mind.

Since these states of consciousness feel so distinctly different, you can easily tell when you are in one or the other. One feels heavy, dull, tight, and contracted, while the other feels light buoyant, inspired, and expanded. One is a state you don't want to be in, while the other is a state you do want to be in. The difference is obvious.

Being aware of and able to identify which state of consciousness you are in is very helpful. This empowers you to shift from one to the other, although doing so isn't always that easy or that immediate. Still, awareness of your state offers the possibility of making some conscious choices about your state, which a lack of awareness does not. Without this awareness, you are likely to stay stuck much longer in a state of consciousness you don't want to be in. So, simply noticing your state of consciousness is a powerful practice. It is what an awake, aware human being naturally does.

Because, even after awakening, you still have the capacity to identify with the ego, or what is left of it, living in the Truth, or being in the flow, requires continually being aware of, being with, and being curious about your experience right *now*. This is not particularly difficult to do once the mind has fallen into the background. In fact, being with what is, is the most natural thing to do. It is what the being that you are has been doing all along.

Before awakening, most of the time, people are not aware of the full extent of reality but of only a small slice of reality—their thoughts. Those thoughts create an imaginary sense of themselves and of life: You create a mental picture of yourself and life, and instead of being *in* life, you think *about* life.

After awakening, because you are no longer involved with your thoughts in the way you used to be, the only thing left to occupy your attention is real life. When your thoughts are relegated to the background, where they belong, everything else comes to the foreground.

When real life comes to the foreground, you notice it like never before. You notice how beautiful, delightful, amazing, and miraculous life is. It appears vibrant, sparkling, magical, and alive, as children often experience life before their egoic mind develops. It is as if someone turned up the dial on your senses, which have been brought to life in more ways than one.

Without a commentator in the background telling you that life is lacking and dangerous, life can be experienced as it really is: simple, joyful, trustworthy, and beautiful. The mind no longer has the power to convince you otherwise, and so you are left with just the *experience* of life, in which you feel your true being rejoicing.

You do not need a voice in your head to tell you how to be in life, what to say, what to do, or how to feel. You have your own experience of this moment. In fact, that is all you have without the voice in your head. Living in the Truth is living in the experience of the moment, where all that needs to be known is known, and all that needs to be done is done. Yes, it is that simple. Life is simple when you are awake to the real reality.

The moment is an ever-shifting mix of physical sensations, energetic sensations, intuitions, insights, drives, desires, urges, impulses, inspiration, feelings, and thoughts. Some of these things come from the five senses, some from the egoic mind, and some from the sixth sense and true self. Any one of those things might be highlighted in a particular moment, as the spotlight of consciousness, or awareness, becomes focused on it.

When that focus is on something produced by the ego, such as a belief, feeling, or self-image, then that often becomes the predominant experience, and the rest of reality is no longer noticed. This wouldn't be a problem if egoic thoughts, feelings, and self-images felt good and if they didn't tend to hijack consciousness as they do. But they generally take you for a ride in the ego's world for a while before they drop you off again in the present moment. And it is not a joyride.

When this happens, it is a bit of a side trip, and like all side trips, you are bound to have missed something by taking it. What you missed is something more pleasant, real, and meaningful. Still, there are no mistakes, only more or less peace and happiness.

Taking a side trip into the mind, or egoic state of consciousness, is like falling into a dream state: You lose awareness of the awake state and all its juiciness and aliveness. Moreover, that dream state can easily become a nightmare if you stay very long. When you are awake, it is natural and normal to slip back into the egoic state of consciousness for brief periods. But it doesn't serve you or life to linger there, except perhaps to remind you of what you don't want to experience.

Living in the Truth is generally an experience of, for example, moving from awareness of a sensation, to a thought, back to a sensation, to an inner realization, to an urge, to an action, to a feeling, back to a thought, then to another sensation, to another action, to an intuition, and so on. When your awareness moves naturally from one object of attention to another without getting stuck anywhere, the experience is that of being in the flow. With each thing you become aware of, you automatically, and usually unconsciously, say yes to it. That yes allows your awareness to flow to the next thing it is aware of and to take any spontaneous action that may also be part of the flow.

Awareness gets stuck when, for some reason, you say no to what you are aware of. Usually this *no* comes from a thought about not liking something, such as how something looks, or not wanting to experience something, such as a painful sensation.

That *no* stops the experience of flow by changing it into an experience of something more like an eddy in which you feel agitated yet stuck. Feeling this way is an indication that you are in the ego's realm and that the ego is trying to not experience what is being experienced or trying to change that experience. As a result, what is now coming out of the flow is thoughts and feelings and a sense of being someone with a problem to fix. This is part of life too, but not such a pleasant part of life.

To move back into the main flow of life, where everything is coming and going and being done effortlessly without any resistance or sense of having a problem, awareness needs to be brought to where the flow has gotten sidetracked into an eddy. If you want to get out of that eddy, you first have to let yourself be in and experience the eddy. The flow has gone there, so that's where you need to be. Trying to be somewhere else only pulls you deeper into the eddy.

If you are caught in the ego's world, the first thing to do is notice you are caught. Sometimes just noticing that is enough to get unstuck. If not, just sitting with the energy of contraction, anger, sadness, or whatever is there might be enough to release the feeling without understanding anything more about that energy.

If just being with a feeling is not enough to release it, then you might need to see how you got caught by examining the thoughts or feelings you are involved with. If this inquiry is able to reveal the falseness or "foolishness" of these thoughts, then the thoughts and feelings are likely to subside, and you will drop back into the main flow.

It can take minutes, hours, or even days for these eddies to unwind, loosen their grip, and release. You have to be patient with this process and continue to be willing to allow and examine whatever thoughts and feelings are present. You are not completely in control of this healing process, and yet you need to allow the process and be present to it as much as possible.

These things have their own timing and cannot be rushed. Once feelings take hold, they are often like a storm that has to run its course. The less you resist the feelings or feed them with more thoughts and feelings, the more quickly the feelings are likely to pass.

These sidetracks into the ego happen because of unhealed conditioning—beliefs, stories, doubts, judgments, fears and other feelings—which needs to be investigated and seen to be false. The conditioning arises because it is time for the mistaken beliefs behind it to be seen and released. This arising and healing of conditioning, which takes place both before and after awakening, is a natural part of one's emotional and spiritual evolution.

Getting stuck in eddies is normal. Accepting this and being willing to let yourself be stuck when that's the experience you are having will help heal and release the conditioning that caused you to get stuck. Emotional evolution is as easy as that. Letting whatever *is* be here and becoming curious about it allows you to keep flowing along with the river of life. Resisting anything that is being experienced does the opposite. Resistance keeps you spinning around and around, like an eddy.

And so the flow goes: Your awareness moves from one thing to the next, from either a sensory experience, a mental or an emotional experience, or a more subtle inner experience, such as an intuition or urge. The extent to which your egoic mind is able to hijack this movement with a fantasy, a feeling, a memory, a desire, or a belief that contracts you depends on how thoroughly you have seen through the false self and its conditioning.

Being hijacked is not a problem but merely the natural process by which human beings become awake and by which they clear the conditioning that interferes with being and staying in the Truth. People do not generally leapfrog from the egoic state of consciousness to perfect freedom from suffering. This evolution generally happens slowly over time, as most people have considerable conditioning, which draws them back into the illusionary world of the false self. Again, this is not a problem or a mistake but a perfectly necessary part of your evolution.

Choice and will are very much a part of this healing process, as the willingness and the choice to be aware, to accept, to be with, to examine beliefs and feelings, and to have compassion for the entire messy business of being human are all choices that bring you more smoothly through this process.

Whenever doing any of these things is difficult, that's just another opportunity to keep choosing to do them. For example, if you are having difficulty accepting something, then just be aware of that lack of acceptance, accept that you are having difficulty accepting, be with that lack of acceptance with curiosity and gentleness, examine your beliefs around the situation, and have compassion for this very human dilemma.

Love yourself and let yourself be however you have been, including how you were a fraction of a second ago. And love others and let them be however they have been and however they just were, as there really is no other choice. Any other choice only causes suffering, because it's already too late for you or them to be any way other than the way you or they were, whether you like it or not.

This love frees you from anything you find difficult or painful. Love what is difficult, love what is painful, love what is scary, love your shortcomings, love other people's shortcomings, love what you love, and love what you hate (what your ego hates). Get the picture? Love whatever is present. That's the secret to life and the secret to happiness. Send love to everything in your experience, which of course includes the ego and its beliefs, desires, discontentment, fears, and other feelings.

This sending of love is a choice, but doing this is so automatic in the natural state that it doesn't feel like a choice. It's just how you *are*. However, when sending love doesn't feel easy and natural, when there is a closed heart and a withholding of love, then choose to love anyway! So what if your heart feels closed, so what if you feel contracted, just notice this and choose to love anyway. The common mistake when one's heart is closed is trying to defend that closed heart with reasons why it *should* be closed. The mind can and will easily come up with reasons to not love, but there is never a good reason to not love, because love is the solution to anything.

When love is your response to a contraction, a negative thought or feeling, or a challenge from life or from another person, that love moves you into the state of consciousness in which healing or a solution is more likely. Negative feelings and challenges cannot be healed or solved from the egoic state of consciousness, which created them in the first place. It only makes sense that you would have to drop out of the egoic state for healing and a solution. When you do that, love is available to do its magic.

The reason that love is the solution to anything is because love is all there is. If everything exists as light, which it does, then light is what you would need to heal something. Love and light are identical. Love is the motivating force behind life, and it appears as light: Light is the form that love takes in creation.

Knowing that love and light are identical makes it easier to see how all motion and activity in life come from love. It's easy enough to see that light is constantly moving. Your cells and the other building blocks of life are always in motion. This motion is inspired by love but appears as light. This movement of love is what creates and evolves all of manifestation.

You know love as the force that draws people together, lies behind the making of babies and all manner of creation, motivates you to care for yourself and others, and draws your attention to something and then to something else. Love is the force that makes something fun or interesting, embraces change, propels you to learn or try something new, and makes it possible to relish a challenge. Every little and big act that you and others perform each day is motivated by this same force.

Even when this force is misguided and misdirected by mistaken beliefs and negative emotions, it is still love, although it is being more narrowly expressed as love for self and self-preservation. Everything people do to survive is motivated by a love for life, comfort, well-being, safety, security, and self, if not a love for others. People may use destructive means to acquire or achieve what they love, but love for whatever they want is still what motivates their actions, although the love is shaped and distorted by the ego's desires and fear.

When you live in the Truth, this love is a real and an ever-present experience. It is palpable. It expands you and fills your heart with joy. It is everything you have ever wanted. And because you know yourself as this love and as all life, this force of love manifests as caring rather than selfishness.

Since love is what has been motivating life all along, when the ego is no longer shaping your life, you still get out of bed in the morning and do whatever needs to be done to support your well-being and survival and that of those close to you. You never needed the egoic mind to motivate you or tell you how to live. You just thought you did, and so this seemed true. The ego took credit for everything that this motivating force—love—did for you, while sending this force off to do its own bidding, to capture its prizes and vanquish its foes.

What is different now that you are living in the Truth is that you do the things you do without resistance, complaints, stories, or having an internal dialogue about them. You do them naturally as they arise to be done: If the phone rings, you answer it (or not); if you are interested in something, you pursue it; if someone asks you a question or asks you for a favor, a response that feels right comes; if you feel tired, you rest; if you feel like being outside, you go outside; if someone needs something, you do what you are moved to do to help, which might be nothing; if something needs to be fixed, you do something about it, which might just be putting it on a list to do when you feel moved to do it.

The answer to what to do and whether to do it arises out of each moment. You never know what you might say or do until the knowing arises. Everyone already knows what living this way feels like, since you have been living like this at least some of the time. Living in the Truth is living this way in most moments instead of in just some moments.

This way of living is completely trustworthy; it is the only trustworthy way to live. The Wisdom that you are reveals itself in every new moment, and the Love that you are moves you as you need to move, always in a way that benefits not only you, but also the Whole.

When you live in the Truth, you are likely to stop doing some of the things that were important to the ego and also some of the things that helped the ego cope with its dissatisfaction, such as overindulgences and escapist pastimes. For instance, you might stop drinking or watching so much television or wearing makeup or seeing friends you no longer have much in common with.

You find yourself pulled to be less busy and to just be, because sitting and just being nourishes you. Just as you naturally nourish your body, you also naturally take time to rest, just be, and do other things you enjoy that feed your soul.

Life becomes less about money, security, success, and being on top, and more about connecting meaningfully with others and with the essence of life, and about creating, learning, and doing whatever else your unique character is moved to do in the world. Maybe that is feeding the hungry or rescuing an animal, but it could just as well be learning to play an instrument, riding a bike, walking in nature, or playing baseball with your children. What this love looks like when it moves is different for every person.

The only way you know how love wants to move in you is to pay attention to how it is already moving in you and moving you. Let love have its way with you. That is all that life was ever meant to be. You are life's unique expression of love, and all you need to do is ask, "How is love moving me now?"

Eventually that question simply runs by itself in the background, and you respond spontaneously to life without consciously asking that question. But until that happens, asking this question and then following the answer to your joy is a choice, the most important choice you can make. Love always knows the way. May you know the depths of this great love that you are, and may it overflow to all of life. Peace!

Book II

*Beliefs, Emotions
and the
Creation of Reality*

INTRODUCTION

That people's beliefs affect their internal reality is obvious and indisputable: Beliefs create feelings, which create an internal emotional environment. What is less obvious is how beliefs affect one's external reality, or the circumstances people find themselves in, which often seem to have little to do with what one believes and feels.

Most people are not aware of the connection between their internal reality (their beliefs and feelings) and what comes into their life. They assume that their inner and outer experiences are unrelated, when they are not. This presumption leads to a false perception of reality. The remedy is to see reality more truly—as it really is, not as the mind assumes it to be.

We are going to explore the exciting arena of creation—how each of you is a creator of your life, or more accurately a co-creator and shaper of it. This act of creation begins with beliefs, is propelled forward by feelings, and is made manifest through actions. Those actions, in turn, cause reactions from others and consequences from life.

The fact that your beliefs create your internal reality and to some extent your external reality is both good news and bad. The good news is that you have the power to be happy because you have the ability to choose what you believe. The bad news is that until you realize that you have this power, your beliefs are likely to make you unhappy, because the beliefs, or conditioning, you were given and those you have acquired along the way largely misrepresent reality. Your beliefs, for the most part, distort and color reality and interfere with experiencing reality as it actually is: You "see through a glass, darkly."

If you are not aware of what you believe and not aware that you have a choice about what you believe, then your life will be shaped by those mistaken and limiting beliefs, and you will be a passive recipient of the results of those beliefs rather than a conscious co-creator of your life. In these pages, we will explore ways of moving beyond any distorted perceptions of reality that may have developed as a result of your beliefs to a truer, clearer, perception of reality.

Each of you has been given and has acquired a set of beliefs that lead to a certain internal and, consequently, external reality. In that sense, you could say that you are programmed with a particular destiny. However, that destiny can be changed and shaped by you once you become more aware of what you are believing and the power you have to believe something else.

Beliefs are potent shapers of reality. It is wise to be aware of this and to become more conscious of what you believe and whether those beliefs are contributing to your happiness and well-being or detracting from that. I am hoping to shed light on this issue so that you are empowered to align with your truest and most fulfilling destiny as a co-creator with the Intelligence behind all life.

Jesus, dictated to Gina Lake
May, 2014

CHAPTER 1

The Illusory Reality

Beliefs create an illusory reality, which becomes one's reality. This illusory reality stands between you and actual reality. Like a pair of colored glasses, this illusory, mind-generated reality changes how reality looks: like clouds, it hides aspects of reality; like a magnifying glass, it magnifies the importance of some things while minimizing the importance of others; and like a funhouse mirror, this illusory reality deceives and makes reality seem scary. Beliefs cause you to perceive things that are not there and to not perceive things that *are* there. Moreover, beliefs cause you to see the world through a singular point of view, the view of "me."

The me that you feel yourself to be is the sense of yourself that is created and upheld by your beliefs. You also have some images, or internal pictures, of yourself, but the sense of you is largely comprised of what you believe yourself to be—beliefs about yourself: "I am this and I am that; I am not this and I am not that. I am someone who likes this and not that."

If you take away all of your beliefs about yourself, you are left with "I am," a simple statement of existence, which is the only absolutely true statement you can make about yourself. If you examine your other beliefs about yourself, you discover that none of them is completely true or true all the time, and therefore none of them is true. Your beliefs about yourself only seem to be true and only seem to be true all the time.

Your beliefs are more like clothing that the "I am" puts on to give it a shape, a definition. This clothing is often necessary to navigate your relationships and activities. You may need to tell someone about yourself: what you do, what you have done, what you like or do not like, or what you want. However, none of these descriptions of or stories about yourself actually defines you or captures who you are, any more than clothing defines a person. Your beliefs give shape to the idea of you and determine how you feel, how you might behave, and what you are likely to do, all of which give further definition to the idea of you. But stripped of all of your beliefs, who or what are you?

When you were born, you were free of all beliefs. You did not even have the concept of "I." You existed as pure being, pure experiencing. You had to learn that you existed separate from your parents and the objects in your environment. You did, however, have many beliefs stored in your unconscious mind from times when you lived before. These unconscious beliefs would be activated and made conscious as you encountered different experiences in this lifetime. But as a baby, your perception was free of beliefs.

As a baby, you saw reality clearly; however, you had no way of organizing and understanding what you saw. As you developed, language gave you a way of organizing the massive amounts of data that your senses delivered to your brain. Language also gave you a way to communicate with others. It allowed you to form relationships, survive, and carry out tasks in the world. What a miracle and gift language is!

And yet, language came at a cost, because with language, came concepts and beliefs. Thus, the sense of "me" was born and the sense of being a separate, vulnerable, struggling entity. With language came the sense of a me in here and everything else out there, and all of the beliefs about "me."

The ego is this sense of being a me. This sense of me is then fleshed out by ideas, or beliefs, about oneself. The sense of self (the ego) dresses itself up in ideas about itself, and a person is born. The person that you think you are is only what you think you are, as there is actually no such thing as a person. What you think of as yourself is only ideas about yourself and a body-mind that seems to be you but which is only a vehicle for who you are. Without beliefs about yourself that define you as a person, you are left simply with am-ness, or beingness, the natural state.

Returning to the natural state, free of the definitions and limitations of beliefs, is what the spiritual journey and human evolution is all about. As an evolved human, unlike a baby, you have a sense of self, which allows you to function independently in the world; however, like a baby, beliefs and self-images don't define you because you know yourself as the am-ness of pure existence. The evolved human being knows himself or herself both as a human being and as divine.

As soon as language develops, beliefs start forming. They are acquired from others and also result from experiences. Beliefs continue to be acquired throughout life and are modified by experience. They can be changed through conscious effort, but most beliefs go unexamined and function behind the scenes as filters and shapers of reality.

These beliefs result in self-images and other definitions of or stories about oneself in relationship to the world as well as countless conclusions about others, the world, God, and life in general. These images and ideas create an illusory reality, which intervenes between you and reality. They become a lens through which you see reality, which distorts and puts a particular spin on reality.

Beliefs create this illusory reality. But it is emotions that flow from the beliefs that make this illusory reality seem real and so convincing. The illusory reality is created by beliefs, but it is strengthened and made believable by feelings. Emotions, because they are experienced physically and not just mentally as thoughts are, make the belief that caused the emotion seem true and important. Emotions magnify and reinforce the beliefs that gave birth to the emotions and also bring their own level of distortion to the illusory reality created by beliefs.

Emotions distort reality by hijacking one's attention and putting the focus on thoughts and feelings, thereby magnifying the mental and emotional realm and minimizing or leaving out other aspects of reality, such as actual sensory input. While thoughts and feelings are an aspect of reality, they primarily create and sustain your personal illusory reality and do not accurately reflect reality. Thoughts and feelings cause one to get lost in the mental realm and lose awareness of what else is going on and what else is true besides what is being believed.

For instance, if the belief arises, "I don't have enough money," feelings of upset naturally follow. Those feelings make this thought seem true, and you become convinced that you really have a problem—because otherwise, why would you feel so upset? Then you start to feel even more afraid and worried, which makes the "problem" seem all the more real and pressing. So, the mind begins to whirl, trying to come up with solutions to your so-called money problem. At this point, you are in a state of consciousness that is not seeing clearly and not noticing the resources you *do* have. You see only what you don't have. You are seeing only half the truth (the half empty glass) and not the whole truth (the partially full glass).

From this contracted, egoic state of consciousness, real solutions are not likely to enter because the state of consciousness that produces solutions is not being accessed. That state would require that you drop all thought, relax, and be in a positive feeling state.

From a contracted state of consciousness, you are also not even questioning the thought, "I don't have enough money." Is this thought even true? Are solutions even necessary? The illusory reality makes a thought seem true, but is it? Where did that thought come from? Whose perspective is it that you don't have enough money? If you buy into that thought, that belief and the feelings it creates will do nothing for you but put you in an unhappy and unproductive state.

What if you didn't believe the thought, "I don't have enough money"? Would you be better or worse off? Does this thought actually serve you or improve your life? Do you need this thought to survive? What does this thought do for you other than drain your time and energy if you believe it? This is the type of examination needed for all of your thoughts.

If you don't buy into that belief or any other, you will simply be present to what needs to be done in your life and you will do it. That state of being present to *everything* that is true in the moment, not just to a belief, is the natural state, and the natural state takes care of itself. If you do not believe that, then examine that belief and those connected to it, because those are the beliefs that keep you tied to the egoic state of consciousness—to the illusory reality created by the ego and other programming.

Taking this example further, if you continue to believe that you don't have enough money and that your mind has the answer to this supposed problem, you will take action in the various directions suggested by your mind: You will get busy doing what your mind suggests you do to solve this so-called problem.

At this point, you may wondering, "What's wrong with that?" That question presumes that answers to how to live your life come from your mind, that is, the thoughts that run through your mind, also aptly described as the voice in your head. If you haven't examined such thoughts, it is natural to believe that the voice in your head has the answers. The thoughts that run through your mind have probably been determining how you feel and what you do your entire life, as such thoughts tend to determine what most people feel and do.

It is wise, however, to examine how well following the advice of your thoughts has worked for you. Has the voice in your head consistently offered good solutions? And do the problems you wrestle with mentally actually exist in reality, or does the voice in your head make them up?

Problems seem to exist, but problems are actually illusory and part of everyone's illusory reality. "Problem" is a concept, not a reality. The mind turns something into a problem by telling you it is a problem. In reality, problems do not exist. You cannot touch, see, hear, smell, or taste a problem or sense it in more subtle ways, because there is nothing there to sense. A problem is imagined.

The most important question to ask in this examination is, "What is the source of my thoughts, and is it trustworthy?" Since there is no answer to where your thoughts come from (you didn't come up with an answer, did you?), then how can you know that your thoughts are trustworthy? Therefore, the only way to know if your thoughts are trustworthy is to examine and question *each* of them.

What is it that is able to examine and question your thoughts? That is a mystery, isn't it? That which is able to examine and question "your" thoughts is the real you. Your thoughts are merely posing as you! Your thoughts are defining a you. However, this is not the real you but an illusory you. Your thoughts create your personal illusory reality, including an illusory sense of yourself and illusory problems. Meanwhile, the you that is able to observe and evaluate your thoughts and see through this illusory reality is who you really are.

The real you uses your intelligence to operate in the world, but it doesn't generally speak to you through the thoughts in your mind. The thoughts that run through your mind day in and day out are the source of your personal illusory reality and your illusory self, the person you think of yourself as, the person who suffers and struggles so with life.

The real you is what is actually alive in you and animating your body-mind. It knows exactly how to keep you safe and unfold your life. The real you speaks to you intuitively and in other subtle ways, not through the commentary in your mind. The real you is also the source of compassion, acceptance, wisdom, peace, contentment, lasting happiness, and love. Every virtue you can name is a quality of your true nature.

Waking up means waking up to the truth about yourself and about reality: You are not who your beliefs tell you that you are, and reality is not what your beliefs tell you that it is. Beliefs stand in the way of experiencing your true self and experiencing reality. Beliefs are all that stand in the way, but that is enough to make this human life a challenge.

To summarize, your beliefs create images (imaginations) and definitions of the person you seem to be, your beliefs define deficiencies and problems that seem to exist, and then the same thing (the voice in your head) that created the illusory self and illusory problems comes up with solutions and advice for how this illusory self should be and move in the world. What a mystery it is to be a human being!

It is no mistake that human beings have a mind that creates an illusory reality, for this allows each person to have experiences that he or she would never otherwise have. Human beings are programmed to create an illusory reality for a purpose: to explore life through a multitude of lenses and to learn and grow from those experiences. An even greater mystery is that you are also divine, and at some point in your evolution, when your personal illusion has begun to dissipate as a result of seeing through it, you discover who you really are, in all your beauty.

The illusory reality's most salient feature is that it has you at the center of it. You are the star in your illusory reality. The beliefs that create your personal illusory reality all relate to you. Even beliefs or thoughts about others are generally in relationship to the me that you imagine yourself to be: how others feel about me or compare to me or are likely to affect me. The thoughts that make up your universe, your personal illusory reality, are in service to the imaginary me. Those thoughts create the me and maintain it. They provide problems for the me to solve, goals for the me to reach, fears for the me to concern itself with, and desires for the me to fulfill.

Whether you are aware of it or not, your mental and emotional world orbits around the me. It may seem like your thoughts are about what you have to do today or what your family needs or what is happening in the world, but the common thread throughout your thoughts is *you*: *your* work, *your* family, *your* world. If your thoughts are focused on others, it is only because you see those people as meaningful in your drama. They are the supporting characters or antagonists in your drama, your movie.

This is not to say that you are selfish and self-centered, only that your thoughts are. This is why one's mental world is ultimately so unsatisfying: It is all about "me." As long as your focus is on the me, you will be constantly searching for satisfaction and fulfillment, because focusing on the me is a place of dissatisfaction and an experience of never having enough and never being good enough.

As you will see in the next chapter, the imaginary me is a set up for unhappiness. As long as you look for the solution to that unhappiness in the answers offered by the voice in your head, you will continue to be unhappy. The unhappiness of the me is only overcome by seeing that the me and its perceptions are illusory and by discovering that there is something else here that has always been satisfied and in love with life just as it is. Until you learn to identify with that mysterious inner joy, you will not be happy, not for long anyway.

This something else that is here is not a better and happier me; it is the experience of no me, of spacious awareness *of* the me and of everything else, with no center, no point of individuation. This spaciousness includes everything and experiences everything as itself. It is the experience of oneself as everything and as nothing at the same time. This is reality stripped bare of all beliefs. This is reality as the mystics know it, and it is reality as you, too, are meant to know it.

Because focusing on the me, the false self, is the source of suffering, striving, and never having enough, once this focus is dropped and you experience yourself as that which is beyond this imaginary me and inclusive of everything, there is great relief, relaxation, peace, contentment, joy, love, awe, wonderment, and fulfillment. This peace and freedom from suffering is the natural state. This is what the me was seeking and, ironically, what the me keeps one from finding. All this was here all along, in reality. Once the illusory reality dissipates, reality shines through, and it is very beautiful.

The spiritual journey is about the gradual and sometimes sudden clearing away of the mistaken beliefs and misperceptions that have interfered with experiencing reality and with experiencing yourself as you truly are. Until some clearing of the illusion has taken place, one's life is focused on the story of "me," "my life," and how the me is doing moment to moment.

The illusory reality created by your mind is much like a movie with you as the central character. That movie tells the story of your trials and tribulations, successes and failures, and ups and downs. In your internal movie, you are not only the central character, but also the narrator and storyteller. Something happens in the saga of you, and a story is told about that: meaning, or spin, is given to that. At every twist and turn, a story is told or a conclusion drawn that relates back to the central character: "That shouldn't have happened (to me), that was wonderful (for me), that was terrible (for me), things always turn out badly (for me), love never lasts (for me), now I will finally be happy, I never get anything right, I've finally made it, nothing will ever be the same, I'm in a slump."

In reality, events happen. Life just happens as it happens. It isn't personal. Who knows why things happen? Life is a mystery that you will never solve no matter how hard you think about it. But the character at the center of the drama gives personal meaning to even the smallest of events, even though there may be no meaning, even though the meaning can never be known.

Stories and conclusions give life a sense of cohesion, and they make life personal—they make life about the central character. These stories, which are based on beliefs and are often themselves beliefs, create a narrative, a storyline. Stories tie together the past, present, and future, giving life a sense of time, which is not inherent in reality. Time, after all, is a mental construct, and mental constructs belong to the mind, not to reality. Only the mind produces concepts and language. Only the mind slices up reality into pieces, labels it, and places it in time.

People's stories not only organize the events in their life into a narrative, those stories also attempt to explain why things are the way they are. Life events are strung together in a story that attempts to explain events or predict outcomes: "That happened because.... When that happens, then...." Such stories are an attempt on the part of the ego to know what it does not and cannot know and to give the character some sense of control over circumstances that are not in one's control. This lack of control over life is very uncomfortable for the ego.

The movie in your head is held together by some kind of plotline: The loser loses, the winner wins, the leader leads, the helper helps. Whatever the character believes himself or herself to be is played out and proven in the story—in life. The character is destined to fulfill that belief.

For example, if your character believes he is fearless, he will be fearless, and that belief will be reinforced. If the character believes she is loving, she will be loving, and that belief will be reinforced. If the character believes he is a criminal, he will commit crimes, and that belief will be reinforced. What the character believes about himself or herself becomes the character's destiny.

Beliefs are more often than not self-fulfilling prophecies. That is why becoming aware of your beliefs is so important. A self-fulfilling prophecy is a belief that is not true but becomes true merely because it is believed.

Here is the way this works: Beliefs shape perception. They cause you to see reality in a particular way by filtering out some aspects of reality, some aspects of your experience, and distorting and magnifying others. This distorted perception—this illusory reality—results in an internal feeling state comprised of interrelated emotions. Those feelings then shape your responses to others and to the world and determine your actions. In turn, those responses and actions provoke responses and reactions from others that tend to reinforce the belief.

For example, take the belief that people are mean. That belief tends to generate an internal climate of anger and defensiveness. Others, sensing and possibly even experiencing these feelings coming from you, are likely to respond coolly to you or with anger. Others mirror back your feelings to you, thereby reinforcing the belief that people are mean.

The perception that people are mean makes it likely that you will notice instances when people are being mean and filter out instances when they are being kind. Or you may assume that people are mean when they are not. Perceptions filter reality in ways that seek to prove one's beliefs. Because the ego has a need to be right, it directs your attention to evidence that supports its beliefs and steers your attention away from evidence that does not support its beliefs.

This creating of reality and learning from what you have created is as it is meant to be. There is no mistake here. Each of you is meant to live out and learn from the beliefs you carry—until a certain point in your evolution when you discover that you have some choice about what you believe and, therefore, about your destiny.

Your beliefs don't have to determine your destiny if you don't want the destiny that your beliefs are creating. You can change your beliefs or detach from and move beyond them. When you change or stop believing your beliefs, your inner reality changes and then external circumstances will follow. You are meant to be *conscious* creators, not just creators. Everyone creates with their beliefs, but gaining control of the creative process by becoming aware of the power of your beliefs changes everything. Your beliefs no longer create your reality—you do, the real you, that is!

Awareness of your beliefs and the power you have to choose what you believe or to believe nothing frees you from your illusory reality and the drama created by your false perceptions. Awareness frees you to create what your heart wants you to create instead of what your thoughts are destined to create. After all, your thoughts have never made you happy for long, but the heart truly does know the way to happiness.

The reason the thoughts that go through your mind do not make you happy is that, for the most part, they come from the ego and unconscious programming, from both this lifetime and others. The ego was not built to generate happiness. Only by learning to detach from the thoughts that run through your mind is lasting happiness found.

When you detach from the voice in your head, all that is left to guide you is the heart. This is not the broken heart that is sung about in love songs but the spiritual heart, the place within the human that receives guidance from its divine nature. This place happens to be located near the physical heart.

The spiritual heart has been guiding you all along, but it is often overshadowed by beliefs. When beliefs stop running your life and the heart takes over, your life will change because you will no longer be caught in your personal illusory reality. You will see all the beliefs and stories that created your illusory reality for what they are, and then you will know reality.

Before closing this chapter about illusory reality, it seems important to define what I mean by reality. Reality is what is left when the stream of thoughts stops or is no longer given attention or prominence. Reality is everything you experience beyond and besides thought and the emotions created by thoughts. This includes:

- *Subtle inner experiences, such as intuitions, insights, wisdom, knowings, inspiration, and drives that come from your true nature;*

- *Higher emotions and qualities of your true nature, such as joy, peace, gratitude, love, compassion, contentment, patience, fortitude, acceptance, wonderment, and awe;*

- *The experience of oneness and connectedness with all that is; and*

- *Sensory experience and the energetic impact of sensory experience within one's being.*

Reality is the pure *experience* of life without the interference of thought. It is pure experiencing, as babies do, but with the awareness and consciousness of knowing yourself as both an independent entity and as a divine expression of life. This experience is one of unity and completion, fullness and depth of love for all creation, an ability to be human and divine simultaneously, to be divinely human.

This wholeness is what you have come to earth to experience, so when you do experience it, you feel completely satisfied. The end of the journey as a human being is to feel this complete, this unified with all of life. And all that is necessary to finally come home, to this place of peace, is a willingness to see through the illusory reality cast by your mind and also a willingness to be still and be present to what is real and true here and now.

Chapter 2

The Ego's Reality

The beliefs that make up both the personal and collective illusory reality are largely beliefs that the ego holds about reality. The ego's beliefs are easy enough to discover because they appear as thoughts that run through your mind. Your thoughts are primarily your ego's thoughts, along with some conditioning, not really "your" thoughts, not the real you anyway.

This simple fact, that the voice in your head is primarily the ego's voice, explains why most people are the way they are and why the world is the way it is: People think they are what the ego says they are, and people behave the way the ego suggests they behave, at least much of the time. Fortunately, many also respond to the deeper cues that come from their true self.

Interestingly, many of the ego's beliefs about reality are quite different from the truth. The picture the ego paints of reality is not accurate and, consequently, leads to unfortunate results and unnecessary suffering. That suffering eventually wakes people up to reality, so there is method in this seeming madness.

Because the beliefs held by the ego are for the most part contrary to the truth about reality, the egoic state of consciousness, which is the state of consciousness of most of humanity most of the time, could be called insane. To believe and act as if something is true when it is not could be a definition of insanity. It could certainly be called delusional.

However, because most people believe the misperceptions of the ego, these perceptions are not generally questioned, and not without a cost to those who do question them. As in the Hans Christian Andersen story "The Emperor's New Clothes," no one dares to tell the truth to the king for fear of being thought to be stupid. The situation humanity finds itself in is even worse than that: Very few even *know* the truth about reality because most don't think to inquire into the mystery that is life, the mystery at everyone's core.

Fortunately, there have always been those who inquired and who realized the truth and were willing to tell it. And fortunately, times have changed. Questioning is rampant. The insanity of the stream of thoughts that goes through people's minds is being exposed, and people are becoming free from the programming that has kept them in a state of unquestioned suffering.

What is the egoic state of consciousness and what beliefs does it rest on? Everyone knows the egoic state of consciousness well, but it may not be thought of as a state of consciousness if you don't realize that another state is possible. For most people, the egoic state of consciousness seems to be just the way things are, the way life is. For most, the illusory reality created by their thoughts is the only reality, and that reality is scary, untrustworthy, cruel, harsh, and unfair. This is the ego's view of reality, and a case can be made for this. However, the ego is ignoring how abundant and supportive reality—life—is.

Why human beings are given an ego that has such perceptions is a subject for another time. Suffice it to say that the programming that is the ego is not a mistake but part of the divine design. The ego not only shapes the sense of individuality, it is also behind the drama in life by creating the inner and outer conflict that drives life forward and provides innumerable lessons, which would not occur without this programming.

Reality only seems scary, untrustworthy, cruel, harsh, and unfair because believing that life is scary, untrustworthy, cruel, harsh, and unfair keeps people from experiencing reality as supportive and trustworthy, although reality is admittedly unpredictable and difficult at times. The belief that reality is scary, untrustworthy, cruel, harsh, and unfair becomes a self-fulfilling prophecy.

Those beliefs become the lens through which people see reality. This lens is the egoic state of consciousness, the illusory reality created by the ego. The feelings created by these beliefs, particularly fear and anger, make the ego's perceptions seem true, and then actions (or no actions) are taken in keeping with these perceptions. These actions evoke responses from people and life in general that reflect back and reinforce the internal state of fear, anger, and distrust.

For example, if you believe that life is scary, untrustworthy, cruel, harsh, and unfair, then you may also conclude that your attitude must be "eat or be eaten, attack or be attacked, look out for #1." If this is what you believe, then the aggressive internal climate created by those beliefs will cause you to behave accordingly. And if that is how you behave, then that's how other people are likely to behave toward you. Then that will become your experience and the experience of anyone else who takes on those same beliefs, which they will if they encounter enough people like you.

This is how a particular state of consciousness can come to pervade a world. One's state of consciousness is contagious: Others start to behave toward you as you behave. If enough people are behaving similarly, the beliefs underlying that state of consciousness are reinforced and become more believable, and the illusory reality created by those beliefs appears true and real.

Egoic beliefs and behavior create a world where people behave egoically. Beliefs manifest as reality. This is why nothing short of a change in consciousness will change your world fundamentally. This change of consciousness is imperative now.

That consciousness is contagious is also good news. Changing the consciousness of a relatively few number of people can cause a snowballing effect, because the truth has an advantage over the ego's lies, since the ego's lies lead only to suffering and the truth to the opposite. Once enough people see the falseness of their thoughts and realize that their thoughts are the cause of their suffering, and once people realize the possibility of a better reality, consciousness can change quite rapidly.

Much of what keeps the ego's lies in place now is the fear of being different from the crowd, of stepping beyond convention and going against how most people think. Once there is less of a stigma around questioning your programming, because more people are not drinking the ego's Kool-Aid, people will awaken to the truth—to reality—much more easily. You are in the midst of and a witness to a revolution of consciousness, right now, in your time.

Here is another example of how the egoic state of consciousness can become a self-fulfilling prophesy: If you believe that life is scary, untrustworthy, cruel, harsh, and unfair, instead of feeling angry and aggressive, you may feel defeated, powerless, and afraid to face life. Many who find themselves in the grip of addictions feel just this way.

Such an emotional climate makes it difficult to summon the confidence, optimism, courage, fortitude, insight, and perseverance necessary to achieve a happy, fulfilling life. Without the necessary internal emotional climate, you are not as likely to go after what will help you to be happy, grow, have healthy relationships, develop your talents, or do what makes your heart sing. You will probably settle for a life of "getting by," one that seems safe but is unfulfilling and joyless, thereby reinforcing the perception that life is unfair and harsh, and happiness is out of reach.

The life that your ego would have you create, as reflected in the thoughts that go through your mind, and the life that your heart, or soul, would have you create are very different lives. Most people follow their heart at least some of the time if they are at all happy. But many do not, and a life of doing only what your thoughts tell you to do is hardly worth living.

You are here for a reason, and that reason is discovered by following your heart, by following your intuition and your joy, not by following the voice in your head. Isn't it amazing that this is not taught to children at an early age and taught in schools? Instead, institutions teach the opposite: Your mind has all the answers.

The stream of thoughts in your mind is not the same thing as your intellect. Unlike the voice in your head, your intellect does not speak to you mentally but is a tool for performing the mental tasks necessary for surviving, creating, and flourishing.

The voice in your head does not have the answers for how to live your life, although it pretends to. For guidance about how to live your life, you need contact with your true nature, your heart, and attunement to your intuition and other subtle means the soul uses to guide each person. Your mind is not who you are. You are a spiritual being. Your mind, including your intellect, was never meant to be the master but the servant of who you really are.

There is so much about reality that the ego does not include in its perceptions and does not understand, making the ego a particularly poor guide to life. The ego's view of reality filters out the spiritual side of life because the ego does not, and will never, understand the great mystery that is life. When something leaves so much of the truth out, it is difficult to call it anything but a lie.

Partial truths just are not true, although something that is partly true may seem true, which is why the ego's perspective on reality does seem credible.

The ego's limited view of reality also seems true because human beings are programmed to believe their thoughts. You naturally believe what you think. You naturally identify the thoughts that run through your mind as "your" thoughts. And being egocentric, as the ego is, you naturally assume that your thoughts are the correct ones, not just for you but for others as well. This egocentricity and undying trust in the voice in your head makes you feel like you know more than you actually know.

The basic stance of the ego and of the mind is, "I know this because I think this." This self-certainty keeps people from looking more objectively at their thoughts and questioning them. If they did, the illusory reality spun by the mind would fall apart. And so it does, once you start taking a good look at the stream of thoughts that seems to be yours.

The ego's illusory reality is one in which the ego believes it knows, while reality is the experience of mostly not knowing, until you do actually know something. What a difference this is! The ego pretends to know things it doesn't actually know just to feel safe, secure, and right. But how safe and secure does it make you to believe that you know something when you don't? The only security that pretending to know brings is a false sense of security.

The ego, as reflected in the stream of thoughts that seems to be yours, pretends to know what is going to happen, pretends to know why things happened, pretends to know what others are thinking and feeling, pretends to know what others are like, pretends to know what is right for others and for itself, and pretends to have answers and knowledge it doesn't have. That is a lot of pretending, all to avoid the painful (for the ego) truth that the me doesn't actually know very much.

The truth about your moment-to-moment reality is that you don't know very much, not nearly as much as you would like to know. Does that make life scary, untrustworthy, cruel, harsh, and unfair? Only to the ego. Only if you believe it does. Not knowing is just what it is like to live in reality instead of in one's illusory reality.

Not knowing something doesn't feel dangerous or scary once you realize that life operates on a need-to-know basis: You don't need to know until you do, and then you do. It is mostly because the ego doesn't trust life that the ego feels it needs to know. When you trust life, you discover that you don't need to know the things the ego wanted to know.

All of that knowing and pretending to know only gets in the way of purely experiencing the here and now, because if you think you know something about what you are experiencing, you will be mentally comparing your ideas with what you are experiencing rather than just experiencing whatever you are experiencing.

For instance, if you think you know someone, then your image of that person will interfere with experiencing that person freshly and clearly, as he or she actually is in that moment. This bringing of the past and other ideas about someone into your current interactions is the cause of most relationship difficulties. Or if you think you know a flower because you know its name or something about it, you will be busy with your thoughts about the flower rather than experiencing the flower. Thinking and experiencing are two very different experiences, different states of consciousness, really. One is a mental experience and one is an actual experience of reality.

When you do examine your thoughts, you discover that they have a dim view of life, of yourself, and of others. The view from the vantage point of the ego is not only fearful, distrustful, and competitive, but one of scarcity and lack: Everywhere the ego looks, it finds lack. When you look out at the world through your ego's eyes, you see and feel that something is missing: in you, in others, in life, and in your experience. You are not enough, others are not enough, life is not enough, and you don't have enough. This sense of lack and never having enough permeates the egoic state of consciousness. The ego is a programmed, ongoing sense of lack, which imagines lack where there is none.

This programmed feeling of lack is one of the reasons people drink, do drugs, overeat, and try to escape reality in other ways. They are trying to escape the ego's painful illusory reality—and who can blame them? They are trying to escape the sense of not being or having enough by filling the imaginary void within themselves with alcohol, drugs, food, sex, and material things. The trouble is, imaginary voids cannot be filled, because they are imaginary.

This egoic sense of lack creates a feeling of having a problem that needs to be fixed, which the ego is glad to offer advice about. The thoughts in your mind send you here and there, trying to fix a problem that only exists in your mind. The fact that other people's minds might agree that you have a problem doesn't make an imaginary problem real, but their agreement does make imaginary problems *seem* real.

The perception of a problem and desires that stem from that problem as well as other egoic desires drive people's activities and make the world as you know it what it is. Everyone is busy trying to fix their perceived problems and trying to get what they believe they lack and therefore what they believe they need to be safe and happy. This sense of lack drives the greed that has been so damaging to many and to the earth.

When you are no longer in the egoic state of consciousness and the ego is no longer driving you, life naturally unfolds. Part of this unfolding is that so-called problems become resolved and needs and desires get met, and if they don't, you discover that you have the inner and outer resources to deal with that. If you don't take on the ego's view of reality, life will still happen, you will still do things, and you will be safe and okay. In fact, if you stop seeing reality through the eyes of the ego, you will stop feeling unsafe and not okay, and you will start feeling genuinely happy and at peace.

Once you have dropped out of the egoic state of consciousness, you experience security, okayness, peace, love, joy, and the insight and wisdom you need to move safely, effectively, and happily in the world. You don't turn to the voice in your head to define you, define your problems, solve those problems, or steer you toward happiness. From your natural state of being, the experience is one of addressing whatever needs addressing moment to moment, of life flowing and unfolding organically, and of life naturally taking care of itself.

The idea that life takes care of itself sounds absurd to the ego. If this sounds absurd to you, and even if it doesn't, this might be a good place to stop a moment and ask yourself what your mind's objections are to this idea. What arguments or reservations does the voice in your head have when you hear that life is trustworthy and supportive rather than untrustworthy and unsupportive, as your ego supposes?

One of the most common reactions the ego has to the idea that life is trustworthy and supportive is to, metaphorically or not-so-metaphorically, get angry and stomp off. The ego doesn't want to investigate the veracity of its beliefs. It tends to attack and belittle the person who suggests that the ego's viewpoint is a lie. This is a defense mechanism, which helps keep the ego in place. Egos don't question themselves. No real self-examination goes on in the egoic state of consciousness, just "I believe it, therefore it is true." This is how the illusory reality is held in place.

Another response on the part of the ego to the idea that life is trustworthy and supportive might be to list all the ways that life does not seem trustworthy and supportive: "People are starving, people are being shot to death over drugs, the economy is in collapse, terrorists are trying to get us, whole species are dying off, the environment is polluted, there are no jobs, the game is rigged against the little guy, you could die anytime."

The list goes on, without acknowledging that (except for the fact that one could die anytime) so many of the things that make life so nightmarish are created by believing what the ego believes. The ego believes there is not enough, so it takes more for itself than it needs. The ego is afraid, so it grabs for power and abuses it. The ego judges people who are different as bad or inferior and uses that as justification for killing or mistreating them. The ego makes the bottom line—money—more important than the well-being, health, and future of human beings and the planet. The ego's selfishness, egocentricity, and belief in scarcity are behind all manner of tragedy and horror on earth.

In reality, people get sick, they get old, they get injured, and they die, just like every living thing. But this doesn't make life unsupportive or untrustworthy. This is just the way life is on earth. The ego doesn't like death, but there can't be life without death. Death makes room for new life. Reality also gives life, replenishes it when it has been destroyed, and provides what is needed for life to thrive. Reality is bounteous, plentiful, unstoppably alive, and ever new. Reality provides everything you need to exist. The proof of this is that you exist.

Reality is also changeable, unpredictable, and unknowable, but this also does not make reality cruel, unfair, harsh, or even scary or untrustworthy, as the ego concludes. The ego's conclusions are incorrect, an illusion. These conclusions create an inner climate of distrust, fear, anger, powerlessness, and hatred, which manifests in reality in ugly ways and is then mirrored back. Then the ego's belief that life is cruel, harsh, scary, untrustworthy, and unfair becomes a self-fulfilling prophecy. In this way, the ego's illusory reality is created and reinforced.

The truth is that reality is completely trustworthy in its changeableness, unpredictability, and mysteriousness. You can always count on reality changing and changing unpredictably much of the time. Reality is not personally persecuting you by being the way it is; the way it is, is just the way of life.

There is nothing inherently untrustworthy about change or about not being able to know what is going to happen. Reality only seems untrustworthy if you equate unpredictability with being untrustworthy. But that is a misunderstanding. Life is trustworthy *and* unpredictable. But because the ego doesn't like the way life is, the ego believes life is untrustworthy and cruel. Like a child, the ego throws a tantrum because life is not the way the ego wants it to be: "Life shouldn't be this way. Things shouldn't change. People shouldn't die. Life is cruel (because it's not the way I want it to be)."

The person who is afraid of or angry with life, who doesn't trust it and experiences it as cruel, harsh, and unfair is overlooking all the ways that life is supportive. How many times have you been down to your last dollar, when all of a sudden something happened to help you out? How many times have you wondered what you would do next, when an opportunity or idea suddenly arose out of nowhere? How many times have you met just the person you needed to meet or found just the book you needed to read? Everyone's life is full of amazing stories, even seeming miracles, in which life brought something unexpectedly wonderful and exactly what was needed.

When you look for such occasions, you will find them. And many people do. These people are happy. They believe in life.

They believe they are partners, co-creators, with something greater than themselves, which is helping shape their life. Life itself is a miracle, and the Intelligence behind life brings you everything you need — and more.

If life is bringing you something you do not want, then that is also what you need. You have to learn to want even that — accept even that — in order to gain from that experience and discover the gift in it. Limitation is a gift; challenges are a gift. Limitation and challenges hone and shape you and make you stronger. Other people harming you can even be a gift if you don't allow such acts to make you bitter or broken.

Even so, most of the hurt and harm in the world is a result of the egoic state of consciousness. When that state of consciousness is no longer the predominant one on this planet, much of the hurt and harm will disappear, and what will remain is an experience of unadulterated reality.

CHAPTER 3

How Beliefs About Yourself Affect Your Reality

The beliefs you hold about yourself are powerful shapers of your experience as well as powerful creators and destroyers of possibilities. How you see yourself and what you believe about yourself are very important. And yet, many people are not particularly aware of the effect that their self-images and beliefs have on their lives even though they experience the results of having those self-images and beliefs.

As long as you are unaware of the images and beliefs you hold about yourself, you will be somewhat of a victim of them. I say "victim" because the images and beliefs people have about themselves are often limiting and detrimental, since those images and beliefs are largely determined by the ego and by conditioning.

Self-images and beliefs about yourself are, at the very least, incomplete, and therefore a lie. They misrepresent you because they are only partly true, since they leave out so much. Anything you imagine or think about yourself cannot begin to capture the multifaceted, ever-changing mystery that you are.

Your images and beliefs about yourself are therefore not worthy of shaping your life, and yet, they do. They limit your life—your possibilities. They steer you in a particular direction, which narrows your opportunities and limits what you are likely to experience.

This narrowing of experience is bound to happen. The real question is: Are you living the life you are meant to live, the life that fits for you—for your soul? Do you even *believe* there is such a thing as a soul or a life you are meant to live? If you don't, how does that belief affect you?

If you do believe that there's a life you are meant to live, is it lived by following other people's advice? Or is the life you are meant to live discovered by listening to your own mind? Or to something else? Do you believe that something else exists to guide you in life besides your thoughts and other people's thoughts? Do you believe there is something called the heart that is meant to guide your life? What does guide your choices? What do you *believe* should be the basis of your choices?

These are very important questions because the answers will determine whether you live according to someone else's ideas, your own, or something else more mysterious, more subtle and yet more real than ideas: your heart.

The trouble with your self-images and beliefs and with following other people's beliefs is that they can cause you to make choices that are not in keeping with your heart, which is the soul's guidance system. Your heart lets you know if your choices are fulfilling your soul's intentions. When they are, you feel joy. When they are not, you feel depressed, unhappy.

If you don't believe this, then chances are you are not following your heart but your ideas and other people's ideas about you. And chances are you aren't happy. The way you know if you are following your heart is whether you are generally happy with your choices. Do you like the life you are living? If the answer is no, your choices probably are not aligned with your heart, or no longer aligned. You are meant to be happy and enthusiastic about life! If you aren't, you probably are not following your heart. And if you aren't following your heart, you are most certainly listening to and believing the thoughts that run through your mind.

People's self-images and beliefs often keep them from doing what they love and creating the life they want and keep them doing what others think they should be doing. This is the source of much unhappiness and depression, which is what living a conditioned life feels like.

People find themselves living a conditioned life, one shaped by other people's ideas or by their own (many of which they acquired from others), because they *believe* they need to please others, or they believe that others know better than they do, or they see themselves as incapable of making good decisions, or they believe they have to obey their parents. And perhaps they don't even believe there is such a thing as guidance from the heart, or they don't trust it. If you find yourself unhappy and living such a life, it can be helpful to answer the following questions:

- *What ideas and beliefs about yourself and about life are behind the choices you've made?*

- *What do you imagine yourself to be now and in the future? Is that who you want to be, or is it who someone else wants you to be?*

- *If that is not who you want to be or how you want your life to be, then what are you afraid will happen if you no longer had those self-images and beliefs?*

- *What would you choose to do if you didn't have those beliefs?*

❖ *What fears might prevent you from doing that?*

❖ *Is it okay for you to go after what makes you happy? Is it okay for you to be happy?*

This is a very important investigation. It can make the difference between a happy life and an unhappy one. The only thing that stands in the way of happiness is a thought, a belief. Beliefs can block you from leading the life you are meant to live and they can make you unhappy even when you are living the life you are meant to live.

All of the ideas you hold about yourself come from the ego or are part of the programming that creates the character you are playing in this lifetime. These self-images and ideas give definition to the individual that you are in this lifetime, and that is purposeful. You are here on earth to experience being this character and to learn to create as this character. That act of creation includes creating a life as this character and developing and shaping this character with your choices.

This act of creation is carried out within the parameters you are given, such as your gender, intelligence, culture, talents, and other capabilities. Within those parameters are lots of possibilities, many of which will be untapped by you and which perhaps are meant to be tapped by you, but beliefs stand in the way of you doing so.

You may already be happy with the life you have created and the character you are pretending to be, but if you aren't, you can learn to create something different. You can learn to *be* different, not by pretending to be different or even by affirming that you are different, but different in the most dramatic way — by waking up out of the character you are playing altogether and allowing your true being to be expressed in your life.

When you are no longer allowing your self-images and beliefs to define you and shape your life, then something else much more real comes to the forefront and moves in you to shape your life—but *it* doesn't have a shape. Who you really are has no self-images or beliefs and therefore no psychological baggage preventing it from moving toward possibilities that once seemed impossible or were not even in view.

This that is shapeless, nameless, and faceless has always been present in the background, molding your life to some extent. Once you are aware that that is who you really are, it can play a more prominent role in what you are creating as the character you are playing.

What might this Self, your true self, create? You don't know until you do. This Self moves without the voice in the head telling it what to do. It doesn't need that voice. *You* never needed that voice! This that you really are moves spontaneously, freely, and joyfully as needed and as inspired. A life created in this way is very different from a life that your self-images and beliefs create. With self-images and beliefs, the focus is always on the me: "What do I want, what do I need, and what will be best for me?" Without self-images and beliefs, you respond to what Life wants, what Life needs, and what will be best for Life.

As part of the Whole, you move according to the will of the Whole, the will of the Father, according to Thy will. When you are aligned with your role within the Whole, your life flows, and opportunities and support of all kinds appear. On the other hand, when you believe yourself to be the character that your thoughts describe, then the life you create is the story the character is telling and learning from: If you believe you will never be happy, you will have that experience. If you believe you have to work hard to survive, you will have that experience. If you believe you have to do what others want you to do, you will have that experience. If you believe you won't ever find true love, then you will settle for something else.

This is all well and good and part of everyone's evolution and therefore does serve the Whole in its own way. But creating as this character is a very different level of creation than what is possible. A higher level of creation is possible once you know who you really are and you have learned to create your life from Thy will instead of the will of the character, the will of the ego. Living in accordance with Thy will is a very different experience than exploring the ins and outs of the small will.

At a certain point in your evolution as a spiritual being, you realize that you are meant to create as the being that you are, not just as the ego that you have. The ego and its will, its beliefs, its fears, its desires, and other conditioning create the character that you are playing. This character experiences many difficulties and much suffering, most of which are created by the character's beliefs. As this character, you are learning how powerful your beliefs are, what those beliefs result in, how they create the suffering you experience, and how moving beyond your beliefs can release you from this suffering. So, your evolution is centered first on learning how to be a better creator as the character you are playing and then, later, on creating in a more fulfilling way as your true self.

There is much value in learning to be a better creator as the character you are playing. Most spiritual and psychological tools are in service to that. These tools support you in becoming a more effective, kinder, and happier character by helping you overcome mistaken and limiting beliefs and replacing those beliefs with more functional ones. These tools include affirmations, visualizations, positive thinking, hypnotherapy, and the whole range of New Age, New Thought, and more traditional healing technologies.

Becoming a more effective, kinder, and happier character is an important aspect of everyone's growth. You can hardly advance to the next level of creating without working on this level first. Some polishing of the rough edges of this character and diminishing of the negativity in your inner reality is necessary before the diamond at the core of your being begins to shine forth.

Once your illusory reality has thinned and dissipated sufficiently, usually as a result of inner inquiry, emotional healing, and meditation and other spiritual practices, your true being begins to be experienced more strongly and more frequently. Then that begins to move you in your life instead of your beliefs and emotions. Thy will becomes more active in shaping your life, and your life becomes an instrument of creation for Thy will. The personality of the character is still there, but it is put in service to Thy will and becomes an expression of Thy will. Your experience of yourself is no longer as the character but as the being that you are.

Spiritual awakening is marked by this experience of knowing yourself as a spiritual being rather than as the character you appear to be, or that your thoughts would have you be. You become free of the illusory self that is created by your thoughts, your programming.

After awakening, the spiritual being that you are operates as the character you have been playing, for that is the vehicle or costume you have been given, which is necessary for navigating life; however, your being is no longer limited or defined by that character and the thoughts that run through the character's mind. Your being remains empty, spacious, shapeless, nameless, faceless, and genderless, while at the same time appearing as a person with distinct likes and dislikes, talents, and foibles. You are a mysterious blend of human and divine!

In the interest of, first, learning to become a better creator as the character you are playing, let's take a look at some examples of how beliefs about yourself shape your life. First, let's consider beliefs around being a man or woman. Each gender is loaded with beliefs and expectations that shape and limit possibilities, often beyond one's awareness. Every culture has expectations for each gender and so does every family. Children are trained from birth to act a certain way, to develop themselves in certain ways, and to see themselves in a certain way depending on their gender. Meaning is given to gender: "I am a woman/man means...." How you complete this sentence reveals the beliefs you hold around your gender, many of which are limiting.

How has your gender determined your choices and shaped your life? You would undoubtedly have had a very different life if you had been born as the opposite sex and not had the conditioning that came with your gender, but then you would have had the conditioning of the other gender. When it comes to gender, there is no escaping conditioning and some narrowing of options.

And yet, your gender is not a problematic limitation from the standpoint of your soul, since your soul selected your gender because that gender could best serve your lessons and purpose for this lifetime. Gender and the conditioning that comes with it is an example of programming that narrows down options and provides challenges but does not necessarily inhibit the soul's evolution. Rather, your gender is part of the soul's evolution. And yet, you can appreciate how even the imprinting of something as basic as gender can profoundly limit and shape your life.

So, not all imprinting and the limitations and challenges it imposes are a problem for the soul and its evolution. However, there is one kind of imprinting that can be very limiting and can inhibit the soul's evolution, and that is the imprint of psychological wounding. This is not to say that emotional wounding might not be part of the soul's plan—grist for the spiritual mill—because it often is. However, emotional wounding is the kind of imprinting that can severely limit one's happiness for lifetimes. So, bringing awareness to the beliefs that underpin any emotional wounding is especially important.

Emotional wounding creates the deepest distortions in one's personal illusory reality and therefore the greatest suffering. Emotional wounding takes the form of beliefs about yourself that create enormous pain and limit your possibilities and therefore the potential for a happy and fulfilling life. Emotional wounding keeps you stuck in the lies your mind is producing and marching to the drumbeat of the ego, which is a drumbeat of fear, negativity, and not enough.

Emotional wounding creates a darkly distorted view of yourself and of life, which spreads its poison to others, often through more abuse or destructive acts. In other words, emotional and physical abuse wounds people emotionally, and those emotional wounds lead to either further self-abuse or abuse afflicted on others. Becoming aware of the beliefs behind the emotional wound frees you from this cycle of pain and hurt.

When you are young, you have no identity; you don't know what to think about yourself. Ideas about yourself are given to you by past-life imprinting, parents, siblings, relatives, teachers, friends, and others close to you when you are growing up. You are told who you are, sometimes directly but often covertly and subtly. Children also draw their own conclusions about themselves based on their experiences. One's identity is made up of ideas collected along the way from all of these sources.

The problem is that once these beliefs are formed, they aren't easily reshaped or erased. And once they are established, they tend to become self-fulfilling prophecies, which reinforces those beliefs. Consequently, what a child is told early on about himself or herself is crucial and will largely determine how happy and fulfilled he or she will be. If the messages were negative, that person will have to work to overcome that programming through awareness of it and a conscious attempt to reprogram those ideas.

Because the illusion is not that easily seen through, this can take years of diligent effort.

If the programming you received was detrimental and limiting, then that is the spiritual work you have been assigned. You are here to learn how beliefs create reality, and that starts with how your beliefs create the reality you are experiencing. If you received difficult programming, it is not a mistake. It is what your soul signed up for to learn to be a more conscious creator. What better way to learn to do that than to first create something unpleasant? Suffering motivates people to create something better or to make the world a better place.

So much growth is accomplished in the lifetimes when you received detrimental programming. In such lifetimes, it is possible to grow by leaps and bounds, which is why a soul chooses difficult circumstances. Such lifetimes are a crash course in creation. If the learning is not accomplished in that lifetime, the learning continues in between lifetimes and into the next. How long it takes is no problem for the soul.

Let's take the example of the belief "I'm not worthy of happiness." This is a very common belief, although often unconscious. It is a real stopper, because whenever you approach feeling happy, your unconscious mind, or the ego, must sabotage that happiness or be proven wrong. Both conscious and unconscious beliefs beg to be proven correct because the ego, which is part of your programming, doesn't like to be wrong. Programming is, after all, programming, and it seeks to maintain itself any way it can.

One of the main ways the programming maintains itself is by filtering out evidence that contradicts the programming. The belief "I'm not worthy of happiness" ensures that you will filter out possibilities for happiness. This might mean that you don't seek out activities or relationships that would make you happy, because if you did, you would prove your programming wrong.

Instead, you are likely to engage in relationships and activities, such as addictions, that don't make you happy, thereby fulfilling the edict of your programming. This all happens, of course, unconsciously, as no one purposefully seeks to create circumstances that will cause unhappiness.

The illusion is very tricky, and one reason it is, is that it is generated and maintained unconsciously. For you to see through your personal illusory reality, you have to become aware of the workings of the unconscious mind and of beliefs that were formerly unconscious. You have to become aware of how you, yourself, and nobody else, is creating your experience of reality and to some extent also creating your external reality by believing what you believe.

The place to start in becoming more conscious of what the unconscious mind is up to is to become aware of what you believe—to become aware of the thoughts that run through your mind. Becoming aware of the beliefs that you *are* conscious of is the first step in unearthing unconscious beliefs—because the beliefs that you are aware of are connected to the beliefs that you are not conscious of. When you tug on the string of a conscious belief, it pulls up, from the unconscious mind, beliefs related to it that you were formerly unaware of.

The best way to uncover unconscious beliefs is to practice observing your thoughts, as is done in mindfulness and other types of meditation, and then to dig more deeply into the limiting beliefs that you are aware of through the technique of spiritual inquiry, which this author has written about elsewhere, as have many others.

This investigation is bound to expose some beliefs that you didn't know were there. In this way, a complex of beliefs that uphold each other, including some unconscious ones, is likely to be revealed. Once this complex of beliefs is sufficiently seen as being untrue, those beliefs lose their power to fool you: Once you have seen through an illusion, as in a magic trick, you can no longer be fooled by it.

Let's take another common belief that holds people back: "I'm not lovable." Other ways this belief might be stated are: "Other people don't like me. I don't like myself. I'm not good enough (to be loved)." This belief becomes a self-fulfilling prophecy in the following way: If you don't perceive yourself as lovable or if you don't like yourself, you feel bad inside. You are living in a negative internal climate, which feels heavy, separate from others, sad, and possibly angry and resentful. Envy and jealousy are also probably present at times.

Such a negative emotional climate makes you feel dark, heavy, negative, and needy, like a black hole. It also affects how you appear to others: You don't smile much, you don't make eye contact, and you keep to yourself. It's like being painted black and makes you almost invisible to others.

If you feel this way inside, others are also likely to sense this about you. If others don't pick up on how you feel by how you appear, then how you feel is likely to be revealed by what you say: You may complain, disparage yourself, judge and gossip about others, play the victim, or drain others with your neediness.

You may not think you are self-centered or self-absorbed, but such a negative internal climate keeps you focused on yourself, your needs, your desires, and what you lack. A negative internal climate keeps you spinning around in your illusory mental reality, the ego's world, trying to fix the way you feel, not realizing that the ways the ego comes up with to fix you won't help. Meanwhile, you aren't very aware of what is actually happening in reality, including possible opportunities or any love and support that may be coming your way.

When you are focused on yourself, you aren't able to be present or loving to others or available to help them. If you were, that would be an attractive, not to mention pleasant, state. When you aren't open and loving to others, then you won't be perceived as very likeable. And if you want their love or anything else from them, they often sense this and move away. The prophecy that others don't love you becomes fulfilled, because the you that your internal state has created is not very lovable. And of course, it is also difficult for you to love yourself when you feel this way, no matter how many affirmations you may repeat.

Even when you don't love yourself, you can have compassion for yourself, which is the beginning of loving yourself and getting in touch with your inner light and letting that shine. Compassion for yourself is the bridge that takes you out of the grip of your personal illusory reality into reality, because compassion is a quality of your true nature.

This is a Catch-22, though, isn't it? How do you find compassion for yourself in your inner darkness? Well, you have to look for it. That's all, really. It *is* there. Compassion is the key. Once you know that it is the key, then feeling loving toward yourself is just a matter of using the key. But that does take a willingness to see the truth about why you don't love yourself and a willingness to use the key.

Here are a few more, simple examples of how beliefs about yourself become self-fulfilling prophecies. If, for example, your self-image is that you don't like to exercise or that you don't like to eat right or that you are someone who adores food, your unconscious mind will do its best to uphold that self-image. One of the ways it does this is through stories: Whenever the subject of exercise or eating comes up, you tell others the story of how you don't like to exercise, how you don't like to eat right, or how much you adore food.

If you don't continue to live up to that image, that will make you wrong, and the ego doesn't like to be wrong. So, if someone says, "Want to go on a hike?" You check with your self-image, see that hiking doesn't fit your self-image, and reply, "No thanks. I don't like to hike." Or if someone says, "I feel so much better after changing my diet. You should try it to," you reply, "No thanks. I don't like to eat healthy food" or "I love food too much to do that." Then you continue to live your life in keeping with your self-image: You don't exercise, you don't eat healthy food, or you put food at the center of your universe—because if you didn't, you wouldn't be being true to yourself, true to your self-image. In this way, you become what you believe yourself to be and what you tell others about yourself. By closing off opportunities to experience yourself differently, your beliefs about yourself are proven true and fortified.

Let's look at one more example of a belief about yourself that becomes a self-fulfilling prophecy and limits your possibilities by creating a distorted, illusory personal reality. The belief is "I'm a failure." This belief could be stated in a number of different ways: "I don't believe in myself. I won't succeed at anything I try. I'm not as good as others, so there's no use trying. I always screw up. I'm not like others—nothing I do works. There's no hope for me."

As you can imagine, this is a very debilitating belief. After all, life is made up of moments of doing, or attempting to do, one thing and then another, often something you have never done before. When you believe you are a failure, then everything you do becomes a test of your self-worth. It is painful to take life this personally, and if you believe you are bound for defeat, it would be easy to conclude, "What's the use of living?" And many feel this way.

The belief that you are a failure becomes a self-fulfilling prophecy for a number of reasons. First of all, this belief creates a negative internal climate that not only feels bad to you, but also feels bad to others and makes you appear unattractive to others. A negative internal climate tends to repel people and opportunities that could smooth your way, just as the belief "I'm not lovable" does.

More importantly, the belief that you are a failure undercuts your motivation and saps your energy, because negative emotions are draining. To succeed, you at least have to try, and usually repeatedly—you have to persevere. "If at first you don't succeed, try, try again" is very sound advice. But unfortunately, those who believe they are a failure often don't even try the first time, much less persevere.

At this point, it seems important to note that success actually only exists in the ego's illusory reality, because success is a concept. It isn't real. There is no clear definition of success, and there never will be. If you do achieve success, your ego won't let you rest for long before it redefines success. Then you are chasing after success once again. You never attain it for long. This is not to say that you shouldn't try to be successful at what you do, only that *you* will never *be* a success or achieve it for long, because your ego constantly redefines what that means.

What is important to your soul is evolving by learning, and learning results from so-called failures. Trying and failing, and trying something else and possibly failing, and trying again and succeeding, and then trying something else and failing is how life naturally unfolds on planet Earth. To your soul, failure *is* success, because that is how learning happens!

When you think of yourself as a failure, you are taking life very personally. Failure doesn't exist in reality, any more than success does. "I'm a failure" is the ego taking life personally. With the ego, everything that happens turns into a story about "me," when in reality, what happens is just how life is happening.

The solution to a belief such as "I'm a failure" is not necessarily to affirm the opposite. Affirmations are often not enough to transform deeply embedded unconscious beliefs, which need to come to the surface first before they can be transformed.

Beliefs are transformed by seeing that they aren't true. You may need to see that a belief isn't true many, many times to become free of it, not just once. You need to do this for as long as a feeling, such as the feeling of being a failure, is experienced. If a negative feeling state is there, then beliefs must be there. If you can become aware of the beliefs behind that feeling state and then investigate them until you uncover the unconscious beliefs that are connected to the conscious ones, then that will release you from the grip of those beliefs and feelings. Of course, part of this investigation is seeing that those beliefs are not true.

With beliefs such as "I'm a failure," the question needs to be asked: "Where did this belief come from?" It is in your own mind, but where did it originate? Who or what put it in your mind? Can you find the origin of that belief? If you look, you can't. This is equally true of any belief that you hold about yourself. You cannot find the origin of any of your thoughts.

You might say that your father put that thought there or that you put it there (in which case you should be able to remove it). But the truth is, that thought and lots of other ones are just there. Your father might have told you that you were a failure, but he didn't put that thought in your mind. It's just a thought in your mind, and it must have been a thought in your father's mind if he said that to you. Who or what put that thought in your father's mind?

Where do your thoughts come from? Are your thoughts or anyone else's the truth? Are your thoughts or anyone else's God's thoughts? Do people's minds speak the truth? With even a superficial examination of the voice in your head, it becomes obvious that the voice in your head is not even close to being the voice of God or the truth. The thoughts in your mind are more like the opposite of the truth than the truth. They are more like Satan than like God.

So, why would you believe such thoughts? The only reason you do is that you were programmed to believe what seem to be "your" thoughts. But they are not your thoughts. Believing that they are is the foundational lie that makes the illusory reality possible.

Those who are successful already believe they are or can be successful even if they don't appear successful at a particular moment. Believing this keeps them motivated and persisting when things aren't going well. They believe that at some point their efforts will lead to success—who knows when? Those who are successful keep the "when" open, never concluding that they have failed just because they may be having difficulty.

Sometimes the only difference between someone who achieves what he or she sets out to do and someone who doesn't is a "can do" attitude, which you might call hope. Optimism and hope create a positive internal climate, which leaves the door open to possibilities and makes manifesting those possibilities much more likely. This begs the question: How might you have narrowed down your possibilities unnecessarily simply by *believing* something wasn't possible?

It's not that those who are successful are successful all the time. They are likely to have had many experiences of failure, but they don't define those experiences as such or let those experiences become the belief "I'm a failure." They don't take their so-called failures personally. They don't turn an event into a story about themselves. Only the ego—the great saboteur—does that.

Here's how the belief that you are or can be successful becomes a self-fulfilling prophecy: This belief creates a positive internal state, which is attractive to others and attracts opportunities. When you believe in yourself, others believe in you, and they naturally want to help or join with you, which makes success more likely and happiness inevitable even if success is not immediate.

Your internal climate is really important! It is like a signal, or vibration, you send out. Those who resonate with that vibration will be attracted to you, and those who don't resonate with that vibration, won't be attracted to you. This means that if you are broadcasting a vibration of limitation, failure, and self-hate, others who resonate to that sad song will gravitate toward you, while those who dance to a happier tune will be repelled.

People with similar internal climates flock together and sing the same sad—or happy—song together, reinforcing each other's internal realities. People live in different realities: Each person is in his or her own illusory reality, surrounded by many who are experiencing a similar illusory reality. And then there are those who live mostly in reality, who have a much better experience of life.

This explains to some extent how people can have such divergent views of life. For example, some see people in general as mean, while others see people as nice. As a result, some people don't like people, while others love people. Your beliefs create an internal state, and that results in a particular experience of reality—a particular reality.

While a negative internal state is created by spinning around in your thoughts and believing your thoughts, a positive internal state results from simply not being lost in the illusory reality generated by thought. When you are present to reality without thoughts and feelings distorting your experience, your internal state will naturally be positive.

A positive internal state is actually your natural state. Your true nature is content, joyful, loving, compassionate, at peace, and accepting. It is naturally alert to reality and notices and responds to what is actually happening without the usual distortion caused by thoughts and feelings. Your true nature is naturally wise and responsive to life. In any moment, it knows exactly what to do and when to do it.

Not letting your thoughts and feelings interfere with your responses to reality doesn't mean you won't use your rational mind when you need it. It's just that people who achieve what they set out to do don't let their egoic thoughts determine their inner climate. They use their mind for what they need it for, and the rest of the time, they are aware of what is being presented in the moment, what is coming out of the flow. The magic of life happens when you are tuned in to the flow, where it is going, and what your particular role in that is. If you are lost in thoughts and feelings, you won't be in the flow and you won't notice the opportunities that come out of the flow.

Your beliefs are not all that is shaping reality. Your beliefs determine your internal reality and affect how you behave and therefore affect reality to some extent. But something much more mysterious is at the helm of life, and it—Grace, or Thy will—is steering life in a particular direction, which I'm calling the flow.

The flow is the direction that Life is taking, and the flow is not up to you. You do not control the flow, although you influence it in small ways. However, you do determine your *experience* of the flow—of reality—mostly by choosing what you believe and by choosing to either accept what the flow is bringing or rail against it.

When you go with the flow, life feels much easier; when you resist it, life feels especially hard. The egoic state of consciousness is the experience of being upset with the way things are, while the flow is what life feels like when you aren't involved in your ego's beliefs, so-called problems, fears, and likes and dislikes.

Sometimes the flow brings success, and sometimes it brings challenges, roadblocks, or what you might call failure. You are not in control of what the flow brings. However, you are in control of whether you are noticing the flow—whether you are paying attention to reality—or whether you are lost in your mental reality. And, importantly, you are in control of your attitude toward what life brings.

If you can maintain a positive inner climate, that will help you drop into and remain in the flow. Then life will feel much easier and Life's opportunities and support will be more apparent. Doing the work of weeding out or learning to detach from beliefs that create a negative internal climate is so important, since such beliefs are what prevent you from being in the flow and, consequently, from tapping into the wisdom and resources you need to handle whatever the flow is bringing.

Chapter 4

How Beliefs About Others Affect Your Reality

As we have seen, your beliefs about yourself affect how you feel about yourself, how you experience others, and what kinds of people you attract. Your beliefs about others are equally important in determining what kinds of experiences you will have with others and in relationship. The beliefs you hold about those around you determine how you will relate to them and how they will experience you. So, let's take a closer look at this great mystery of how you create your experience of others and, consequently, your experience of reality.

Your beliefs about people in general as well as your beliefs about specific people shape your experience of them. As for people in general, what is it you believe? Do you believe people are mean or nice? Do you believe they like you or not? Do you believe they are trustworthy or not?

And, of course, you believe different things about different groups of people: You have beliefs about poor people, beliefs about rich people, beliefs about children, beliefs about teenagers, beliefs about Christians and Jews, beliefs about Americans and every other nationality, beliefs about the different races, beliefs about women, beliefs about men, beliefs about the elderly, beliefs about attractive and unattractive people, beliefs about intelligent and not-so-intelligent people, beliefs about overweight and thin people, and on and on. That's a lot of beliefs to be aware of and examine!

No matter how the mind divides humanity up conceptually, the ego has an opinion about those people, and it believes its own opinions. Do you see how artificial these groupings and boundaries are, how they are made up by the mind? How can opinions about imaginary groups be anything but imaginary—not real, not true?

And isn't it interesting how your mind has an opinion about everyone and every group—instantly! That's what minds do: They form opinions instantly, and you instantly believe your own opinions. Opinions are beliefs, and like beliefs, opinions often go unquestioned and unexamined.

Any of your beliefs can and will shape your behavior toward someone, especially if you are not aware of your beliefs and their effect on you. The more aware you are, the less your beliefs unconsciously shape your behavior. And since beliefs can be especially destructive to relationships, the less your beliefs interfere in your relationships, the better it is for everyone. Unconscious beliefs limit your ability to behave flexibly and respond naturally and freshly to the person in front of you.

Your beliefs limit your choices about how you behave. For instance, if you don't trust men, you will behave as if you don't trust them instead of in the many other ways you might if you did trust them. You won't be free to be more open toward a man, which is more functional than being closed. Being more open and trusting doesn't mean you won't be discriminating and careful, because if you are very present to what is actually happening in the moment, your intuition will let you know if you are safe with someone or not.

The ego's beliefs are its rules for how to live. The trouble is that the ego's rules and formulas don't take into account what is actually happening. Approaching every situation with the same set of rules and formulas is not going to give you very good results; and yet, that is what living according to your beliefs is like. Living this way is like wearing the same clothes every day of the year no matter what the weather is like. Just as you adjust your clothes to the temperature, you have to adjust your behavior to the present moment. If you are living in your illusory reality instead of reality, you won't make those adjustments.

Sometimes men can be trusted and sometimes they can't, to return to our example. The belief that men can't be trusted is untrue because this only applies to some men. A belief that is true only some of the time is hardly going to be useful in guiding your behavior.

The mind loves to lump people in categories. It's simpler that way. It's also just how this primitive aspect of the brain, the ego, works. It sees things as either black or white, good or bad, trustworthy or untrustworthy, with nothing in between, even though even the simplest of things, not to mention human beings, is multifaceted, complex, and mysterious.

Your beliefs about others not only limit your flexibility with others and your ability to be with others freshly in the moment, but also create a particular experience of reality that reinforces your beliefs. Just as beliefs about yourself become self-fulfilling prophecies, so do beliefs about others.

Let's take a look at how the belief that men can't be trusted can become a self-fulfilling prophecy. If you are a woman who doesn't trust men, you will expect men to treat you badly, lie to you, hurt you, or betray you. If you feel this way inside, you will be looking out for yourself in whatever relationship you are in. You will be on guard, and love won't be flowing easily from you to the other person.

If that's the case, then love is not so likely to be flowing toward you either. Or if your partner is expressing love, either you won't be able to receive his love or it won't register. Your filtering system will notice the times he isn't being attentive or the ways he seems untrustworthy, not the ways he is.

Because your ego wants its beliefs upheld, your unconscious mind might even compel you to do and say things that are unkind and cause your partner to withdraw or be unkind in retaliation, without realizing your role in this. If you are unkind, insecure, defensive, or cold in relationship because of some belief, that inner climate is bound to sabotage your chance for a healthy relationship. Who you are likely to end up with is someone who is willing to be with someone who is unloving, insecure, defensive, or cold because he needs to be with someone—anyone—rather than because he loves *you*. This can't be a satisfying relationship for long, and your belief becomes a self-fulfilling prophecy.

Alternately, if you distrust men and therefore expect men to treat you badly, you are likely to accept such a relationship. Here is how that works: If you believe that men treat women badly, but you don't want to be alone, you will accept bad treatment from someone because that will seem normal. When you don't expect anything better from a partner, you will accept the behavior that you expect because you don't expect to find a man who treats you well.

This happens all the time in relationships. If you set the bar low and don't expect to be loved and treated well, you will settle for a relationship that has very little love. On the other hand, if you expect to be loved and treated well, you won't stay with someone who doesn't love you and treat you well. This is how beliefs limit and shape people's relationships.

Your expectations and beliefs can limit possible relationships and cause problems in your relationships in another way: If you require that another person look or be or act a certain way before you will love him or her, you are greatly limiting your chances for love. Finding someone who meets your specific requirements will be difficult, if not impossible. And if you are already in a relationship, your expectations and ideas about how you want your partner to be will only cause conflict between you.

You just can't win with beliefs! Whether your expectations are high or low, they will cause problems, because life is not designed to meet your desires and expectations. Life has its own purpose and its own plan. Life brings you the people it does for many reasons, which you may never understand. Your only choice is whether or not to love who Life brings you.

The mind has its ideas about how relationships should be and how others should behave, but these ideas only create suffering for everyone. Love is possible only when you drop all ideas and beliefs and meet another just as he or she is showing up in the moment, fresh and new. Any ideas you bring into that moment about that person or about anything else will only interfere with experiencing that rich, unique moment with that person.

Love is experienced anytime you are truly present to the person in front of you without any ideas, beliefs, or expectations. Love is not the result of getting someone to fit your ideas or finding someone who does. If you wait for life to fit your beliefs and desires, you will be waiting forever.

Moving beyond your beliefs about others allows you to experience them as they really are. Then it is possible to feel the love that naturally flows between one being and another when beliefs no longer impede that flow. Love is your true nature, and only beliefs stand in the way of experiencing your true nature and someone else's, because beliefs keep you in the ego's illusory reality.

Some beliefs can override or counteract ones that limit or inhibit love. They are beliefs that would come from your true nature if it spoke to you, as the voice in your head does. Such beliefs reflect certain universal principles and truths. Here are a few examples:

You are a unique and precious expression of the Divine. I honor and respect your uniqueness. How you are different from me is a gift and as it is meant to be.

You are lovable just the way you are. You don't need to change for me to love you.

You are not in this world to fulfill my needs or for my purposes but for your own purpose, which I honor and support.

You have your own lessons, and I support you in making your own choices and learning what you need to learn from them.

Any belief or idea that allows love to flow within you and within those you are relating to is a belief that is very close to the truth about life—close to reality—and therefore can be helpful in counteracting the untruths the ego produces.

Some beliefs are truer than others. The closer your beliefs are to the truth about life, the more you will feel the peace, love, joy, gratitude, and contentment of your true nature. A test of how true or useful a belief is, is whether it blocks love or allows love to flow. Beliefs that contribute to the ego's illusory reality interfere with love and make you feel bad and contracted inside, while beliefs that represent life more truly allow love to flow and make you feel good and expansive inside.

The more time you spend in the present moment without your thoughts, the more you are able to know life as it truly is, as your true self experiences it. If you spend enough time being fully present in the moment, you discover the truth about life—that it is good, trustworthy, wondrous, miraculous, and divinely and intelligently guided. Only your personal illusory reality keeps you from realizing this. Your beliefs cause you to misperceive life. Once the lens of your perception is cleared of the beliefs that distort your vision, you can see life as it really is.

Beliefs like those just listed override the ego's erroneous beliefs and take you to the *experience* of the truth. They point to something that is not a belief but rather a universal truth, which when realized, results in peace, love, and harmony within you and in your relationships. That is how you know something is true—because it results in peace, love, and harmony. That is the test. If you apply this test to your beliefs, you will see that not many of them pass the test.

You don't need your beliefs! What a radical idea that is. Your beliefs only get in the way of reality, which is the experience of peace, love, and harmony. That is what reality is! Just that. Reality is the experience of peace, love, and harmony.

Let's delve a little more deeply into how your beliefs about others affect your reality, because seeing the truth about your beliefs frees you from the damage they do to your relationships. Yes, seeing the truth is enough to free you. Nothing more is needed. But there is a lot of examination to be done, since the mind is full of lies and partial truths.

Your beliefs and ideas about the specific people in your life have an enormous impact on your relationship with them—as do their beliefs and ideas about you! More often than not what makes or breaks a relationship are the beliefs and ideas each person has about the other and about the relationship, rather than compatibility or other factors.

If you have positive beliefs and ideas about someone, you will be open to that person, and love will flow easily. But if you have judgments about someone, those will taint your relationship and interfere with seeing the good in that person and with loving him or her. Based on this, you can imagine how many more opportunities for relationship someone who is not judgmental has than someone who is.

Judgments are the number one reason relationships feel difficult, fail, or never get off the ground to start with. And every single one of your judgments is made up by your mind. It wasn't handed down to you from God, because God is the antithesis of judgment, despite how God is sometimes portrayed. Your judgments come from a darker place, a primitive place.

If you are having a problem with someone, you need to examine where the problem lies. Is it in the other person or in your own judgments? Perhaps the problem also lies in the other person's judgments. Without judgments and stories about someone, is there a problem? There may be differences that need to be worked out, but the mind often creates unnecessary problems.

Some important questions to ask about your judgments and beliefs about someone are: "Is this always true or just sometimes true? Is the opposite also sometimes true? Do I really know this about this person or am I assuming this? Am I just pretending to be able to read this person's mind?"

If you investigate your judgments and beliefs, you discover that the mind makes a lot of assumptions and pretends to know things it doesn't actually know. The ego does this because it wants to feel superior and right. It also does this because it loves to tell stories that cause problems and stir up emotions. The ego loves drama, and it doesn't trust love, so it does what it can to sabotage love.

The more important question is: "Is it helpful to the relationship to assume whatever I am assuming?" Judgments come from the ego and are in service to it, so questioning your judgments and their value in general is important. Once you see how useless and damaging judgments are to relationships, you will quickly learn to disregard them.

That judgments close hearts should be pretty obvious. Judgments come from a closed heart, so naturally they also cause others to close their hearts. Judgments are a perfect example of an internal reality, or climate, determining one's external reality. When you openly judge others, you will be judged in return, as predictably as the night follows the day.

Even if you keep your judgments to yourself, the internal climate created by your closed heart will result in others closing their hearts to you, even if they don't know why your heart is closed: Like attracts like, judgment attracts judgment, a closed heart attracts and causes closed hearts, not open ones.

Let's take a look at how the judgment "You don't pay enough attention to me" can become a self-fulfilling prophecy. This judgment, like all judgments, closes the heart, both of the person who holds it and of the person who receives it. The last thing that the person who receives this judgment wants to do is give the person the loving attention he or she is demanding — prophecy fulfilled! Judging someone is a really poor strategy for getting what you want. Judgments backfire every time.

Even if you don't say, "You don't pay enough attention to me," your closed heart, alone, creates the experience of not having enough love. No one else but you can actually make you feel love or feel loved. That is solely up to you. Love is an experience that happens within you. It is an experience of your heart being open. If your heart is open, you won't need love from another person. It's only when your heart is closed that you feel a need for love from another. In holding this judgment, "You don't pay enough attention to me," you create the very experience you are complaining about — a lack of love.

Judgments close the heart and leave you bereft of love. But you do this to yourself. As long as your heart is closed, you will never get enough love from someone else to satisfy you. You can have your judgments or you can have love. But you cannot have both.

If you have beliefs about your partner that keep your heart closed, you might as well not be with that person, as love will eventually disappear unless you move beyond those judgments and begin to affirm something more positive about your partner. Relationships cannot survive ongoing judgment. Even one judgment held by one person strongly enough can destroy a relationship.

Fortunately, since any judgment is just an idea in your own mind, you can do something about that judgment before it distorts your perception of your partner and damages your relationship irretrievably. You can catch your judgments when they form and say no to them. This is one of the secrets of those in happy relationships: The individuals don't engage in judgment, either secretly within themselves or within their relationship.

Does this sound too idealistic? Not engaging in judgment is just good emotional hygiene. Just because most people believe their judgments are useful and not harmful doesn't make them so. Judgments are useless and very harmful, and the more people who realize this, the better. If people understood this and practiced non-judgment, it would dramatically change the world you live in. There is no room in relationships for judgment because judgments leave no room for love.

Everyone has faults, or you could say lesser strengths. If you dwell on someone's weaknesses or so-called faults, then that is all you will notice. So if, for instance, you have the belief that your partner is lazy, and you feed and strengthen that belief by giving that thought your attention, you will begin to see your partner from the "he's lazy" lens and not from any other perspective. His other qualities will be overshadowed by the image that he is lazy.

Your unconscious mind will look for ways to prove this belief and filter out evidence to the contrary.

The mind doesn't acknowledge the whole picture in the stories it tells about someone, and when it focuses in on a negative trait, the relationship can take a turn for the worse. What you give your attention to really matters! If you are going to focus on a belief about your partner, focus on one that enhances love. This is what people in successful relationships do. They tell positive stories about the person they are with: "He is such a wonderful person. He does so many things well. He is always considerate."

Now, he may not *always* be considerate, but when you believe this, you notice when he is considerate and filter out when he isn't, because your unconscious mind wants your beliefs to be right! Having positive beliefs about your partner supports love and helps you overlook the things you don't like. Having negative beliefs about your partner does the opposite: They undermine love and keep you focused on what you don't like. It's so important to be aware of the beliefs you have about others and to keep them positive.

Focusing on someone's positive traits is not hiding your head in the sand. Rather, doing this counteracts the mind's tendency to focus on the negative, which creates problems where there are none. The problems created by judgments and negative images of someone are illusory problems, not real ones. Judgments and negative images break apart relationships unnecessarily. Relationships are challenging enough without causing more difficulties and conflicts by holding detrimental beliefs and judgments. Watch your thoughts about your partner and be careful what you believe.

What are the stories you tell about your partner silently to yourself or out loud to your friends and to your partner? What subtle negative images do you hold of your partner in your mind's eye, and how do those images affect your relationship? This is the illusory reality you create and live in with your partner. And your partner has his or her stories and images about you that create his or her illusory reality, which your partner lives in. These illusory realities produce much unnecessary enmity, conflict, sorrow, guilt, and pain. Change your inner reality, and the outer will follow.

Chapter 5

The Past, the Future, and Now

People talk about the past and the future as if the past and future actually exist somewhere, as if they are a place you could visit, when they are nothing but ideas—in one case memories, and in the other case, fantasies. The past is completely gone, and the future you imagine never arrives. All there is, is one unfolding, ever-changing moment, which is outside of time. Some have called this "the Now," and so will I.

Time is a construct of the mind that is very useful in your day-to-day life, especially for purposes of communication. But like all mental constructs, people's understanding of time doesn't accurately reflect reality. However, because the brain processes reality in a way that creates a sense of time, you cannot escape the perception of time and everything that comes with that.

A number of illusions contribute to making time seem real. One is, as just mentioned, that the past and future feel like they exist somewhere—perhaps over the rainbow? The past and future seem real, solid. And because the past seems real, it often continues to have an impact on the ever-unfolding Now.

If the past didn't seem so real, it would leave no trace and simply be forgotten, like a boat that leaves no wake, no sign of where it has been. But your so-called past does leave a wake; it leaves memories. That is all that remains of the past, but that is something, and something that must be reckoned with.

If memories didn't carry an emotional charge and a sensory component and something else much more mysterious that makes your memories personal, your past would feel no different to you than a movie you just watched. You would be able to forget your past as easily as a movie, and there would be no residue to heal or release.

But memories have something that movies don't, which makes them personal: They are *your* movie, your story, not just a story about someone else. The same magic trick of the mind that creates a sense of being the character you are playing also gives this character a past that matters to the character—and ideas about a future.

The character you are playing not only lives in the Now, but also inside a story that includes ideas about the past and future. The character is made real by this sense of a past and future. Without a story about this character that takes place over time, the character would not exist. The character is living a story with a past and future. The me is the star of an ongoing drama, with a beginning, a middle, and an end, just like in a movie. If you take away the character's past and future, you wouldn't have a story or much of a character, because the character gains its identity from the storyline.

This is how it is meant to be. You are meant to live out a story. This story is full of sorrow, struggle, pain, and success and glory too. It is a grand story. Everyone has an amazing tale to tell of failure and triumph, love and hate, loss and new birth. You cry, you laugh, and you experience every possible experience and emotion over your many lifetimes.

And yet, the character and the story are an illusion. There is no character and there is no story—only the ever-unfolding Now, appearing as a character living out a storyline. What an excellent magic trick! That is what an illusion is, isn't it? It is something that appears to be something other than it actually is. You are here living your life, and you are also not who you think you are. You live in two different realities, an illusory one and a real one: You live as the character and you live as your essence, stripped bare of the costume and script.

Another quality of the illusion of time is that what happened in the past seems really important. The past seems not only real, but also significant. This is why people share their pasts with each other, embellishing and fleshing out each detail for all to hear. But all they are really sharing is their particular story about the past, because the past, itself, can never be shared, since it is gone. All you have are *memories* of the past, the residue, a shadow of something that happened.

That's all that is left, and that isn't much. Memories are not at all like an experience, and they do a poor job of representing an experience. All that memories are is someone's version of something that happened in the past—a story. All you have of the past is your story about it.

The memories people most cherish and dwell on are either their painful ones, in which they felt victimized, unhappy, or unsuccessful, or their happy ones, which make them feel sad because whatever made them happy is no longer happening. Such are the memories people lug around, which pass for the past. The unfortunate thing is that, by dwelling on their painful stories, people wound themselves again and again.

If memories are mostly painful, what motivates people to focus on them and share them? The answer is that stories give the character a sense of existing and definition: "I am someone who lost my mother at eight. I am someone who went into the military. I am someone who had four children." Your stories tell you and others who you are, that is, who you think you are. They give the real self, which would otherwise be unclothed, some clothing. They turn the real you, which is nameless and shapeless, into somebody.

Stories are important to the ego, which drives the character, because stories create the character. Whenever you talk about yourself, you can feel the push of the ego behind the sentences that begin with "I." To maintain the existence of the character, the ego needs to talk about itself. This is why people share their stories with others, and this is why, in their quiet moments, people think about their past. It seems important to do so, and everyone else seems to agree and to be doing the same thing. What kind of a person would you be if you didn't care about your past or other people's pasts? (Much happier!)

If the past didn't seem important, the past would be easier to forget and not so hard to heal from. These two qualities—realness and importance—give the past a dimensionality, an intensity, and a power that it does not deserve.

The past seems like much more than just a thought—a memory—even though that is all it is. It seems like more than a thought because the past is embedded not only in your mind, but also in your body. You carry your memories with you wherever you go, like belongings that you cling to, as if they were so precious—especially the painful memories. Those are even more dear to your heart than the happy memories.

You hold your memories as treasures, and this is also part of your programming. This sense of preciousness ensures that the stories will keep being retold, which contributes so importantly to the illusion of time. So, you see, you are programmed to suffer. It can hardly be avoided, until you begin to see through the illusion cast by your programming.

The seeming importance of what happened in the past drives the character's drama forward. The past, or really the character's stories about it, causes the character to do things he or she would not do if the past didn't seem so real and important and if the stories didn't seem true. The past and, in particular, the stories about the past give the character identity and a *raison d'etre,* a reason to do what the character does.

The character is shaped by what happened in the past and the conclusions drawn about what happened. Those conclusions influence the character's present and, consequently, the character's future. The character's stories about the past determine the character's destiny along with the character's beliefs. The past and the stories related to it are imprinting, just as beliefs are imprinting. If you don't see the effect that your stories about the past are having on your current behavior, you can't be free of that behavior, just as you can't be free of the effects of your beliefs until you realize their effects.

Overcoming the power of the past and the power of your stories to determine your present and your future is largely a matter of seeing that the past is *not* real and *not* important and that it is completely gone. It is also a matter of realizing that any stories you tell about the past are incomplete and therefore false. For most, the past shadows them, shaping how they relate to others, how they feel and behave, how they see themselves, and what they envision as possible and not possible for themselves. They are controlled by a shadow—by something that isn't real.

What happened in the past is responsible for many of your beliefs, so freeing yourself from those beliefs requires seeing the truth about the past. The truth I am referring to is not the truth about what happened, although that can sometimes be valuable. But more valuable than that is realizing that the past is not important.

What happened in the past might have been important then, to that Now, but it is not important to this moment—unless you make it so. You make the past important by believing it is important and by keeping it alive through stories. Believing that the past is important becomes a self-fulfilling prophecy: When you believe that, you hold on to your memories and stories about the past, and those stories create feelings. Then that inner climate shapes your behavior and determines how you experience reality and how reality responds to you. In that way, you fulfill the prophecy that the past is important. The past can only become important if you allow it to.

If you let go of the past, you won't miss it. Memories and stories of the past do little for you or for your life except keep you living out the character's programming. Letting go of the past is not as hard as it may sound, because the past is already gone. (How can you let go of something that's gone?) All you have to let go of are your thoughts and stories about the past, which have rarely served you anyway.

Most of your thoughts and stories about the past fortify the false self. And you don't need that. You can still play the character you are meant to play but without your programming determining the script. Instead of following your programming, you learn to improvise! In place of the script is the flow, the ever-unfolding Now. You learn to do and say what comes out of the flow to do and say.

To realize that the past is not important deeply enough to be free of it requires some inquiry into your own memories: How do you see yourself in the past? What memories have you repeatedly shared with others or dwelled on? What have you concluded from those memories, and how have those conclusions (beliefs) shaped you? Do you need those memories? How might you be different without them? Can you imagine what you would be like or how you would feel if you didn't have those memories?

Your memories, just like your beliefs, create an internal climate that determines your present moment experience. Running those memories in your mind is like running a sad movie in the background while you go about living your life. How can that be helpful? Even a happy memory running in the background only keeps you from fully experiencing the Now. A happy memory can never fulfill you or be as rich an experience as the present moment is when you give the present moment your full attention.

In reality, there is nothing but this fresh, new moment. What will you do with it? Can you approach it anew, like a baby? Can you approach the people in your life as if for the first time? Can you experience the clean, clear, empty, unbaggaged self that you really are?

To the ego, your real self is not as juicy or exciting as the character with all the character's emotions and drama. The ego wants nothing to do with reality or the real self. In each new moment, the ego attempts to pull you back into your thoughts, back into the character and its story.

If you perceive your true self through the ego's eyes, you won't be interested in the peace and love that your true self has to offer, and you won't even realize what it has to offer. You won't get to know the real you. You won't know the shining reality that exists, in which *you* exist. But it is there, waiting for you to discover it.

The future is as unreal as the past, but it is easier to see this about the future than the past. Unlike memories, no one shares their detailed fantasies of the future with others as if they believe those fantasies are real. Nevertheless, most people spend a good deal of time imagining the future, and they hold these ideas dear, as if they were real. People's dreams are important enough to them that they feel angry if their dreams are challenged and hurt if their dreams aren't also believed in and supported by those they love. Many a relationship has ended because the two people involved did not share and back each other's dreams.

There is nothing wrong with having hopes and dreams, but it is good to also be aware that you made those dreams up and that you don't actually know what will be, and to realize that you don't have much control over what will be. The ego doesn't want to admit how little control it has over the future, and it pretends to have much more control than it does.

The ego has a strange relationship with the future: It both fears the worst and imagines the best. There is no middle ground with the ego, only black and white: horrors and dreams-come-true. To the ego, the future will either be terrible or wonderful. You will be either a bag lady or a millionaire.

Just as memories from the past are programmed to feel real, important, and precious, so are fantasies of the future. One of the ways that fantasies are made to seem real and therefore believable is that they have you in them! It is *your* future. You imagine yourself in your dream house, driving your dream car, being with your dream partner. This may sound obvious, but an imagination is greatly empowered when you are part of it. Just as your memories have you at the center, so do your fantasies of the future. This makes your fantasies, like your memories, seem real, important, and precious.

This explains why people don't like their dreams dashed by others or by events. Your dreams are very personal. You are identified with your dreams. Your dreams *are* you. Who would you be without them and without your past? Exactly. That's the point. Your future and your past together create the you that you think you are. Having your dreams threatened feels like a threat to you, and so it is—a threat to your *idea* of you. Only in the illusory reality can someone else's ideas about your idea of your future threaten the idea of you. What a tangled web the illusory reality weaves!

Another way imaginations of the future are made real and believable is that they have elements in them that are already part of your reality. For instance, in your fantasy, you might still live in the same town you are in but in a more expensive neighborhood. Or you imagine that you are with the same partner, but you are traveling the world. Or you imagine that you are driving your same friends around in your new luxury car. You don't imagine yourself in someplace like Oz, where everything is unfamiliar. That would be too strange, too impossible. You would know for sure that that was a fantasy, an illusion. But if your fantasy has familiar elements, that makes it believable and seemingly possible.

Perhaps what most lends realness to a fantasy is the fact that you want it to be real: "I want it to be this way, therefore it will be." People are programmed to believe that their desires will come true. In the end, you believe you will finally get what you want. That is the happy ending everyone longs for. That is the basic fantasy: You get what you want. End of story. But in reality, there is no end of story, except perhaps death, and that is hardly the fairytale ending people are looking for.

When does your happy ending arrive? When your first child is born? Then he gets sick and has to go to the hospital. So, is the happy ending when he gets better and comes home? Then he grows up and is unhappy. What if that doesn't change? Where's your happy ending? Meanwhile all the other ups and down are happening: in your career, in your marriage, in your health, in your friendships, in your finances.

Life is not a fairytale. It is also not a nightmare. It is both to the ego but neither to your real self, which is enjoying the wild rollercoaster ride called life. The ego's idea of life and reality just doesn't fit reality, and that can only cause suffering. The ego wants a happy ending, or a lot of moments that feel like a happy ending. But the ego doesn't ever get the life it wants because that would be impossible. Life is not something you order up from a menu. It doesn't comply with your wishes and commands.

Because the ego has impossible expectations, disappointment is an ongoing experience in the egoic state of consciousness. The character is constantly disappointed by life, even by very simple day-to-day experiences: Your husband brings home the wrong kind of ice cream, you break one of your favorite bowls, your daughter gets a bad report card. Every event in life is an opportunity for the ego to be disappointed, as it compares real life to its fantasy of how life could or should be.

That is the problem with fantasy and future expectations. Life doesn't live up to them, so they cause disappointment with life, when life is perfectly fine as it is. Life is unfolding exactly as it is meant to. To define this unfolding as wrong or not good enough is to tell a story about life that is simply untrue, and untrue stories, as we have seen, only make you unhappy.

Because of how you are programmed to relate to both your memories and your fantasies, you are bound to suffer. The deck is stacked against you as long as you remain in the ego's illusory world. It is a world of pain and suffering, which creates more of the same.

So, how do you break out of the ego's illusory world? An illusion only needs to be seen through before it ceases to be an illusion. But the illusory reality, because it shows up in so many ways in every moment, has to be seen through again and again. Your life must become a practice of seeing through the illusion to the truth in each moment until that practice becomes automatic and no longer needed.

There is no more worthwhile endeavor than seeing through the illusion, but the will to awaken from the illusory reality has to be strong enough to take on this practice. That will comes from the Father when the time is ready in terms of your evolution. Reading this may mean you are ready. If not, then reading this is certainly making you ready. You cannot read this and not be changed by it, because once you see the truth, you cannot *not* see it. The bell cannot be unrung. Your interest in awakening has brought you this far, whether you even realize what awakening is or why you are reading this.

There is no more important practice than meditation for breaking the domination of the ego and its instrument, the voice in your head. Much has already been written about meditation and other practices that facilitate awakening by this author, so I will refer you to those writings. But please know that meditation is the key to learning to live in reality rather than in the illusory reality created by your thoughts and feelings.

The reason that meditation is the key is that it teaches you to be present to—to pay attention to—reality rather than lost in your thoughts and feelings, which create and uphold the illusory reality. Meditation brings you into the present moment, the Now. It gives you a taste of another possible way of being and living as a human. It gives you a taste of your essential self, your true nature. Once you have had enough tastes of reality to trust it, you won't want to return to your illusory reality—and you won't be able to because you are no longer ignorant of the Truth.

So, here is the Truth: There is no past, there is no future, there is only the ever-unfolding Now. Whatever you call the past is the step you are in the midst of taking, and whatever you call the future is also the step you are in the midst of taking. The past and future are contained in the step you are taking *now*. The past and future do not reach beyond this one step except in your imagination. All you are ever doing is taking one step. But the experience of that step is always fresh and new, because it is as if that step is taking place in a moving river, which brings to you all manner of experience.

This river is the flow of life. Life comes to you, and you receive it, experience it, and respond to it. This is the experience of being in the Now. It is effortless, enjoyable, interesting, and wondrous. You feel as if you are moving through life, but it is more like Life is moving through you and moving you. In this way, the water of Life nourishes and sustains all life.

When you are outside the flow of life, in the desert that is the ego's reality, it feels like you have to struggle just to survive. It doesn't feel like life comes to you but like you have to make life happen through your own efforts. When you are outside the flow, the illusion is that you are pitted against life, while the flow is an experience of being beloved and held by life. In the flow, you experience life's bounty and Grace, not the ego's limitation and fear.

The Now is the experience of being held and supported by life, which is the truth. You *are* being held and supported by life. You are not separate from the life force that sustains you. You *are* this very life force. It flows through you and moves you to speak and act, whenever your speech and actions are not being coopted by the ego. You only *feel* separate. But that is the illusion. How you feel does not reflect the truth about reality. Reality is bounteous, trustworthy, and intelligent beyond imagination.

Chapter 6

A Belief That Takes You Beyond Beliefs

As mentioned earlier, some beliefs are truer than others. The more closely a belief matches reality, the truer it is. Beliefs that match reality can be useful in breaking through the spell cast by the illusory reality.

One of the most powerful beliefs for doing this is the belief "I don't know." This belief is nearly always true! Most of the time, you don't know much: You don't know what is going to happen, why something happened or is happening, or even what exactly did happen. You don't know what other people are thinking and feeling. You often don't even know what you are thinking and feeling! Any answers you think you have only cover a sliver of the truth. They are only part of the story.

There is so much that you don't know, that it is difficult to even claim that you know something. When you do claim to know something, what you think you know is usually only part of the truth, and partial truths are just not that true. For instance, you might think you know what your spouse is like. But you still don't know what it is like to be your spouse or what it is like to be your spouse here and now. Like everything else, your spouse is constantly changing, whether you are aware of that or not.

How can anyone possibly know another human being, when that person doesn't even know himself or herself? And yet, people often pretend that they know others, even people they have barely met.

You could argue that you know some fact, like what day of the week it is, your name, or what the weather is like right now. But all you know is a word for the day of the week, a word for yourself, and a word for the weather. The words people use are just labels for things or for concepts created by the mind. There is actually no such thing as a week or weather; those are just useful concepts. And a name for you is not you; it is just a label. Knowing the name of something is not the same as knowing something.

What do you really know? Can you think of anything that you can say that you know? About the only thing you do know is that you exist. You are conscious of existing. But what that mystery of existence and consciousness is, you cannot begin to know.

The value of seeing how much you don't know is that it counteracts the ego's assertion that it knows so much. The illusion is largely created by pretending to know. That is what beliefs are—pretenses at knowing. You pretend to know what is best for other people, you pretend to know what is going to happen, you pretend to know what happened in the past, you pretend to know how you and others should and will behave, you pretend to know what is right and wrong, you pretend to know what other people are like and how they feel about you. The list goes on.

The ego pretends to know things it does not, cannot, and will never know. The ego does this because knowing makes it feel safe, even if that knowing is incomplete or incorrect. Pretending to know is one of the ego's survival strategies, and this strategy serves to some extent. For instance, it's useful to pretend that the sun is going to come up tomorrow, as it seems to always do. Expecting *everything* to be constantly in flux would make it difficult to function, and that would be a lie anyway, since there is a certain stability to your world. And yet, you don't really know that the sun will come up tomorrow or that you will be alive to see it. That's the truth. The truth is that you don't know even very basic things.

The trouble with pretending to know so much when you don't know—with having so many beliefs that don't match the truth—is that doing this keeps you in the illusory reality, where you will look for confirmation of those false beliefs and find them. When you believe that you can know even when you can't, you will keep turning to the mind for answers, and the mind will continue to define you and define reality for you—falsely. You will base your life and actions on pretend knowings, on beliefs, on half-truths.

The truth can only be found in reality. And the experience of being in contact with reality is that you don't know. If you aren't willing to not know, you won't want to spend time in reality. To live in reality, you have to be willing to make peace with not knowing. This is not easy for the ego. So, the only way you can make peace with not knowing is to not be identified with your ego but identified with your vastness, with this great mystery that you are.

Your vastness doesn't need to know more than it needs to know. The ego wants to know so much more than it needs to know! If you knew in your heart of hearts that life is unfolding as it is meant to and that your life and every other life is in good hands, that everything you have experienced and are experiencing is what your soul intended, then would you need to know what is going to happen next? Would you need to know very much at all?

The ego thinks it needs to know so much to be safe and happy, but what if you are as safe as you need to be, as safe as your soul intends you to be? What if you could just relax and let everything be as it is? Wouldn't you be happy then? Isn't that what everyone is looking for, in all their accumulation and one-upmanship? Isn't everyone just wanting to be safe and comfortable enough to be able to relax and just *be*?

You won't find out how little you need to know if you don't spend time in reality. The ego's illusory reality is self-reinforcing. You don't discover what else is possible unless you venture out of that reality into Reality. The big leap from the illusion to reality is made possible by being willing to not know: to not know where the money will come from, to not know how you will accomplish something, to not know why something happened the way it happened, to not know what your life is going to look like or who you will be with. You have never known these things anyway. You have only been *trying* to know and pretending to know, assuming that you needed to know. But you don't.

Let Life come to you. Let Life take care of life. Leave life up to God. Your life and all life has always been up to something larger than you, something of such vast and inscrutable intelligence that it is hard to believe what is, in fact, true. You are in good hands, the best of all possible hands.

Relax and know that you do not need to know for your life to work out. And know that whatever you *do* need to know, you will, when you need to know it. Relax into not knowing. Life is much simpler that way. All you have is this ever-unfolding Now, and all you need to do is be open to fully experiencing the flow of life as it comes to meet you. Let it wash over you, move you, speak you, dance you, love you, and be you. Peace!

Book III

Love and Surrender

INTRODUCTION

This third book in the trilogy, more than the other two, is about the spiritual Heart, the fountain of unconditional love, which was central to my teachings two thousand years ago. The other two books are important in understanding the power that the conditioned, or *egoic*, mind has in preventing people from experiencing this love that is at the core of everyone's being.

Choice and will are what make it possible to move out of the negative and limiting beliefs of the false self, which prevent or curtail the possibility of living a fuller, happier, and more loving life. This book, *Love and Surrender*, explains what is necessary to be in the Heart—in one's divine Essence—and to live from there rather than from a more contracted ego-bound state of consciousness. Surrender is the mysterious thing that happens when one lets go of, or gives up, the perspective and beliefs of the false self for the true self. It is the "miracle" I have spoken of in other works of mine.

My message today is the same as in times gone by: You are not only human but divine, and you are meant to flourish and love one another. You are no different than me. The gift the Father gives each of His children is the gift of His own divinity. He does not give it to only one son, but to all, even those who know Him not. He gives this gift freely and indiscriminately.

Love is the answer today, as it has always been, but love is more important than ever before because today you have the means to destroy this beautiful earth and all that live upon it. The obscurations to love need to be vanquished so that you can abide in peace on this planet. This is more imperative than ever, and so I have come to deliver this simple message of love. May you receive it in your heart and express it in your life.

Jesus, dictated to Gina Lake
October, 2014

Chapter 1

What Is Surrendered

Love and surrender are words that are often used in spiritual teachings. However, like so many words, what they point to cannot be expressed or contained in words, and so love and surrender are often misunderstood. When people think of love, they think of romantic or familial love, which is an emotion, a feeling. But the love I will be speaking of is more mysterious and pervasive than a feeling. This love is the ultimate in human attainment, while at the same time ever-present and therefore beyond any need for attainment, for you already have it.

Although ever-present, this love is often obscured, and therefore so often seems out of reach. It is here, though, and what is more true is that it is all that is here. This love is the vast sea, or ocean, of consciousness from which everything arises and of which everything is made. The love that I am describing is not only the substratum of life, but Life itself—God (if you will).

Love and surrender are important because they bring you your deepest heart's desire as a human being. You are meant to be happy, to love, to be at peace, and to be free. Those are the tasks, you could say, of these human lifetimes. You are meant to move from fear, hopelessness, anger, victimization, and hate to trust, strength, courage, joy, peace, and love.

This transformation comes about through surrender. All of the spiritual practices ever invented are designed to accomplish this one thing. Surrender is the boat that takes you from one shore to another, from the limited human experience to the experience of the Divine incarnate.

Surrender is the means by which you come to know Love, or God. Surrender is mysterious and often *not* something you do, but something that just happens when you cease doing certain things and cease efforting. As a result, surrender often happens when you don't expect it, when you are not trying to surrender and your attention is elsewhere. To some extent surrender is Grace, but a grace in which you play a part. You set the stage for Grace/surrender to happen. You invite it (intend it or pray for it), make room for it in your life, and recognize and allow it when it does happen. That is what you can do.

Because surrender is so mysterious and so critical to spiritual freedom, peace, happiness, and love, we are going to examine what surrender means, what is involved in it, and what is actually surrendered.

When people hear the word surrender, they usually think of one side surrendering to another in a war. The side that has surrendered has been defeated and disgraced and has lost something important, such as territory or rights, and those who have surrendered might be imprisoned or in some other way punished for having lost the war.

The surrender that I am referring to—spiritual surrender—has the opposite consequence, since spiritual surrender leads to gaining something, not losing something, and to greater freedom and happiness, not imprisonment and shame. In fact, what is lost and given up in spiritual surrender is imprisonment, limitation, fear, conflict, and suffering. Who wouldn't want to surrender under those circumstances?

The trouble is that spiritual surrender *feels* like you are giving up something you want and need for something unknown, uncertain, even scary, or for something that seems like nothing. Spiritual surrender *feels* like you are about to lose something even though you are about to gain something. Feelings sometimes lie! The trouble is that you don't discover what you have gained until *after* you have surrendered. Until then, surrender feels difficult.

Surrender feels difficult because you are attached to what needs to be surrendered, if only because it is the known, the familiar, even if it makes you unhappy. You cling to it out of habit. You don't want to surrender it. You struggle with surrendering it. Besides, what else is there?

What are the things that people struggle with surrendering that block them from love? Feelings, for one. You don't want to let go of your anger, your resentment, your hatred, or even your guilt, your shame, and your suffering. And yet, you don't know why you don't want to let go of these feelings. You just don't, and you may not even ask why.

Not wanting to let go of such feelings doesn't make sense, but the part of you that doesn't want to let go of a feeling is not rational. It doesn't choose based on what makes sense. It feels the way it feels, and it is attached to feeling this way, even if doing so doesn't make sense, even if doing so hurts and hurts others.

This irrational side of people is often what runs them, and it keeps them from questioning the thoughts and feelings that cause their suffering. Most people remain in the dark, letting their unconscious minds determine their choices and inner state. They are unwilling to shine the light of awareness onto their inner landscape.

In addition to their feelings, people also don't want to surrender their ideas about themselves and others, their judgments, their stories about the past, and their fantasies. People like these thoughts, or at least a part of them does, the less rational part. These are the thoughts that make you who you *think* you are—who you believe you are—but not who you *actually* are. They are also the thoughts that make you suffer.

It doesn't even occur to most people that they need to surrender these thoughts in order to be happy and more loving. No one else seems to be doing this either. Most people don't realize that these thoughts are the source of their suffering, their imprisonment in a small, limiting definition of themselves. Most people remain ignorant of their greater self, their true self, and so they huddle fearfully inside this shell created by their ideas about who they are, not realizing that they are in prison, not realizing what else is possible.

But you who are reading this do realize something that most others do not, or you wouldn't be reading this. You realize that life is meant to be richer, fuller, happier, and more loving. You realize that you can be happier and more loving, if only.... If only what? If only you are willing to surrender the familiar prison for the unfamiliar palace.

Before you can surrender what imprisons you, you have to realize that you are in prison and that a palace awaits you. That realization ignites the necessary willingness and conditions for surrender that take you from prison to palace, from fear to love, from limitation to happiness and fulfillment.

Surrender is essentially an exchange. You surrender the old for the new, since the two cannot coexist. One cancels out the other. Surrender cancels the old and makes it possible to discover something new. But first, the old must be surrendered. The old must be given up, let go of, and only then can you discover what takes its place.

Surrender requires faith that something will take the place of what was surrendered and faith that what takes its place will be better than what was given up. Usually, this faith comes naturally when the old way of being creates sufficient suffering.

I say "sufficient," because enormous suffering is often endured before most are willing to consider a new way of being, one that hasn't been modeled for them, one not taught in schools, a way of being that is different from the way most people are living. Very few are courageous enough to step outside the usual way of being without good cause, and that cause is most often deep suffering.

It isn't easy to go against the grain. Fortunately, there are more people today who are willing to do this, and those people are able to find and support each other in ways, through the internet and other means, like never before. So, something else that must be surrendered is concern for what other people think, for their opinions of you. The madding crowd keeps everyone in line.

Most people are willingly, yet unconsciously, imprisoned and not looking for a way out. They are the waking and walking dead, going about their lives as they always have, following the rules, not looking within, not questioning the situation they find themselves in, not questioning why they and everyone else seem to be suffering. Their perspective on life is like everyone else's, and that perspective is good enough for them. It is the perspective of the ego, the false self.

For these individuals, spiritual surrender is not the issue because they don't realize the need for surrender. Their questions are: "How can I get more of what I want? How can I get so-and-so to do what I want? How can I get people to like me? How can I get...?" Their questions are about getting something for themselves, not about giving up something (surrender), least of all giving up their suffering and the self that needs and wants things for itself.

What such people don't understand is that everything that is of true value is gained through surrender and remains out of reach by refusing to surrender. This statement doesn't even make sense unless you realize what spiritual surrender refers to. You surrender the false self for the true self. You surrender one state of consciousness to gain another state of consciousness. You surrender your attachment to what causes you to be unhappy and unloving in order to become happy and loving.

This raises the question: What causes someone to be unhappy and unloving? Some believe that their happiness lies outside themselves, that it is caused by people, events, and things. But if you believe that, you are doomed to unhappiness, since you can never control people, events, and things enough to ensure your happiness.

This is also simply not true: Happiness is not dependent on people, events, and things. But most have to discover this for themselves. You are the maker of your own happiness; nobody and nothing else can make you happy. And you are the one who determines to what extent you experience love in your life.

No one and no thing can make you feel happy, and no one and no thing can make you feel love or loved, at least not for long. You have the power within you to be happy and be loving, just as you have the power to be unhappy and unloving. Surrender is what takes you from unhappy and unloving to happy and loving. So, let us look more closely at what needs to be surrendered for this transformation to take place.

Most essentially, the "I" must be surrendered. It must be laid at the feet of the Father. You offer the "I" up (surrender it) to God. This could not be done if there weren't something here capable of doing this, which is the true "I," the true self. The true self offers up the false self, and in so doing, becomes free of the false self and the suffering it creates.

The false self is every idea you have about yourself, every *thought* that begins with "I" and every other thought that relates to "I." Yes, every one. The true self has no need for such thoughts. It just is. It is what is alive in you and experiences life. The true self has no need to define or limit itself with words, while words are all the false self has.

The false self is nothing but the words that it describes itself as: "I am this, I am that, I am not this, I am not that." The false self is a limited self: Some definitions are included, while others are left out. This is not the experience of the true self of itself, which is boundless, all-inclusive, and without definition. Anything you might say about the true self would be incomplete and therefore untrue.

Before you understand this about your true nature, you must experience this for yourself. Some experience of the spacious, all-embracing nature of the true self is necessary before the false self can be surrendered. Even then, this surrender is an ongoing, moment-to-moment process, a moment-to-moment choice. As long as you are human, you are never really finished surrendering.

In every moment, the false self coexists with the true self. The false self exists as thoughts about yourself, while the true self exists as the experience you are having, including the experience of thought. Thoughts put you at the center of the universe and make the universe about *you* instead of you *being* the universe, which is more the truth.

When you become involved in your thoughts about yourself, you are involved with the false self; when you are not, you drop into the pure experience of the moment. The sense of "I" drops away and you become the universe. When you let yourself be nothing, you realize yourself as everything. These are two very different ways of being!

Experiencing the moment without involvement in thoughts about yourself and your life allows you to know your true nature. If you stay in that experience long enough, you will feel love, peace, contentment, beauty, gratitude, awe, and joy, because that is the true self's experience of life. But since few people are able to stay mentally quiet long enough to experience the depths of the true self, these moments of beauty and joy tend to be fleeting, while the experience of absorption in the self-centeredness of the false self is most people's ongoing experience.

Identification with the false self would not be a problem if living as if you were the center of the universe were a pleasant and effective way to live your life—if it worked! But it isn't and it doesn't. That state of mind, the state of identification with one's mental commentary, with one's ego, generally produces an experience of life that is quite the opposite of the true self's experience of life: Instead of peace, your thoughts create anger, conflict, and confusion. Instead of love, your thoughts create blame, hatred, jealousy, envy, and resentment. Instead of joy, contentment, and gratitude, your thoughts create discontentment, unhappiness, greed, and envy. These two states—the state of consciousness that is the false self and the state of consciousness that is the true self—are worlds apart. Surrender is the bridge that takes you from one world to the other.

To make this leap from one world to another, something else must be surrendered: fear. Fear is like a guard at the exit door of the false self's world: Whenever you approach the door that leads to the world of the true self, you are told that you can't go there. Fear is the guard that keeps you in your place, a place of compliant, unconscious suffering.

Fear masquerades as a guard, as someone who is trying to protect you from what is beyond the door, from the unknown, but he is actually the warden who maintains your imprisonment. He keeps you from the Father's palace, while pretending there is something terrible on the other side of the door. It takes courage, trust, and faith to surrender this fear and walk past the guard.

People are also kept in the false self's world by their desires. These are the baubles dangled temptingly before you, designed for your pleasure and for keeping you happy amidst your suffering. But the happiness they deliver never lasts for long, hence the need for another desire and another. There is no end to the false self's desires, since the false self is never satisfied.

Fulfilling these desires keeps people busy and keeps them from looking within and questioning their suffering and way of life. Chasing after one desire and then another keeps you occupied and pretending that you will be happy when.... People exchange happiness *now* for discontentment and striving and the promise of happiness in the future. The false self's desires are designed to keep you on a treadmill of activity, always reaching for something ahead, while missing the beauty and perfection of life as it is unfolding right now.

Surrendering the desires of the false self does not mean surrendering all desire, however, as deeper desires drive the true self. The true self's desires are felt quite differently than those of the false self. These deeper desires are what is surrendered *to*. You exchange the false self's desires for truer, more meaningful ones. You surrender to a higher desire, a higher will.

These desires are the will of the Father, not the will of the ego. You exchange your personal will for Thy will. When you do that, your activity and actions become joyous, fluid, balanced, and kind to yourself and others. You are freed from creating negativity and therefore, for the most part, from experiencing negativity. And whatever negativity you do experience does not affect you as it did in the past.

Once you have put your life and actions in the hands of the Father, your hands are free to give of yourself and to enjoy all that you do. They are no longer tied to unfulfilling activities out of duty to conformity and other people's expectations. The Father's bidding is always good and brings happiness to all. This is a different world, indeed, than that of the false self.

The final thing that must be surrendered is what you think you know, for to enter the Father's palace, requires that you be naked in the moment, free of all pretense of knowing who you are, who others are, what will be, why things were as they were, and why they are as they are. When you are stripped this bare, then it is possible for you to know what cannot be put into words and to have access to everything you need to know—for that moment.

Chapter 2

Surrendering the "I"

If you pay close attention to your thoughts, you will quickly see that they revolve around "I." Most thoughts are about yourself or are being thought because they have some importance and relevance to "I." Most of the time, what goes through your mind is a dialog between you and you about you or things of interest to you. You are very important to you!

Even thoughts about others ultimately relate back to you and your relationship with them: How do they feel about you? How do they or did they affect you? How will they affect you when...? What do you like or not like about them? What do you think of them?

All of this rumination related to you creates a sense of yourself in relation to others and to the world. This sense of yourself is what I am calling the false self. It is, after all, just a *sense* of yourself. It isn't anything more than that. It cannot pick up your groceries or put your kids to bed.

Something else is actually living your life, doing all the things necessary to sustain your life, and that mysterious but very real something does not need a sense of yourself to do those things. In fact, as you well know, that sense of yourself could be very different from what it is right now and you would still exist and do things.

That sense of self is infused, or colored, by ideas, beliefs, and images and connected to a particular body-mind, all of which further flesh out this sense of self, making it appear more solid and real than it actually is. This sense of self seems so real and its ideas, beliefs, and images seem so true that it influences what you do, how you do things, when you do them, and if you do them at all.

But that sense of self doesn't have to affect any of your activities or how you live your life. On some level, it is a choice to have your sense of self affect your existence and your activities to the extent that it does. What a radical idea that is! It is, of course, completely natural for that sense of self to influence your life. Human beings are designed to have a sense of self that seems to be real and seems to be who they are. They are designed to play the part of a specific character, although that character is not who they really are.

Nevertheless, do you see that there is some choice in how much and in what way that sense of self affects your life? Your life, after all, is yours. You are not the character, and your life does not belong to the sense of self. The sense of self is just a sense, and it can change. It can even fall into the background, in which case, the real you, the one that is living your life, will barely be influenced by it.

Ideas and images, which is essentially what the sense of self is, can only affect you to the extent that you allow them to and to the extent that you are unconscious of them. You don't necessarily let other people's ideas affect you, but when those ideas come from your own mind, that is a different matter. Those seem real and true—they seem meaningful to *you*. But they are only meaningful in that they create the false you, a pretend you, a mirage that seems like you.

This wouldn't be a problem if the sense of self and all of its ideas were not also the source of human suffering, because many of the ideas are negative, limiting, and simply untrue and because the sense of self, itself, is false. How can a false self and false and limiting ideas lead to happiness, peace, and love? Lies can only lead to suffering and take you away from the truth. And so they do.

The problem with the false self is that it keeps you from recognizing your true nature and the truth about life, both of which are good news. The false self keeps you bound within a certain perception, one that causes suffering. The false self sees the world from a lens of fear, distrust, lack, and competition. It is essentially an unhappy, discontent, egocentric, and fearful self.

Something else is here that is much more than just a sense of yourself and all the ideas that go along with that. It uses the body-mind to get about and accomplish things, but the body-mind would be useless and inert without it. What is this mysterious thing that is alive within your body-mind, sensing through it, and moving it about? That is the true self. It is called by many names: the Divine Self, Essence, Spirit, Consciousness, Awareness, the Holy Spirit, Being, the Higher Self, and the Pearl Beyond Price, just to name a few.

The title of this chapter, "Surrendering the 'I,'" points to the possibility of not allowing the sense of self—the false self—to shape your life and determine your choices but allowing something else that is real and much wiser and more loving to shape your life, something that has already been shaping your life to some extent.

This mysterious something—the real you—allows your life to be shaped by the false self and its ideas until you wake up to the realization that you are more than this. How momentous this is, when you first realize that you can wake up from the prison created by the false self and live more from the indwelling Spirit! And what a great mystery this business of being human is! What wakes up? What sees the truth about who you are? Who are you? What are you?

As I said earlier, before you can be released from the prison of the false self, you first must realize that you are in prison. Getting to that point takes three things: willingness, awareness, and choice. You have to be willing to look (so many are not!) and then you have to actually look. You have to choose to turn the spotlight of your attention onto something that most people don't want to look at or don't bother to look at: their own mind.

Isn't it interesting that the objectivity that is felt to be so important in observing the outer world is rarely turned in on one's own mind? Rarely do you run across someone who suggests doing this. Even psychotherapists who ask their clients to look within usually assume that a client's thoughts and feelings are a true representation of who he or she is, without acknowledging that such thoughts and feelings are part of the mirage of being human and must be looked beyond to discover the real truth. But there is a place for that kind of examination, of course, and this is by no means intended as an indictment of psychotherapy.

As long as the sense of self is felt to be the real self, the experience of the real self will be only fleeting and not recognized. The real self will remain in the background, unacknowledged and therefore not experienced as such. Of course it is impossible to not experience the real self, because the real self is what is reading these words and experiencing life. It is the only thing that is experiencing and can experience life.

The human condition is such that people assume that something else is the real self. They assume that the false self is the real self, that it is the experiencer, the wise one, and what acts. The reality is that the false self (your thoughts) only pretends to be wise and to know things that cannot be known, while true wisdom flows from the depths of the real self and is overlooked by the false self. And actions, which could come entirely from the real self are often determined by the false self instead, which barks out commands and seeks to control your every behavior: "Do this now. Do it better. Hurry Up. You'll never get it done in time."

Much of the commentary that goes through people's minds is a chain of thoughts designed to get them to take action in directions that will yield greater power, control, safety, security, pleasure, recognition, and comfort, all things the ego esteems. There is nothing wrong with these things, but there is much more to life. The false self doesn't know how to create a happy, loving life. The life it creates is lopsided and detached from what brings true meaning to life.

Through some kind of mutiny, the egoic mind (the voice in your head) has become the captain of this ship of the body-mind, while the real captain has been sequestered down below. He has been replaced by a less capable captain whose guiding principles are fear, power, selfishness, and control. This false master is not a good master. He is not wise and he is not kind. Reinstating the wise and kind master so that love and right action can reign once again on board is the goal of spiritual evolution.

Surrendering the "I" is impossible without first recognizing the need for surrender. You have to have clearly seen the ineptness and destructiveness of your thoughts. This takes not only awareness of your thoughts, but also the willingness to examine and question them.

Surrendering the "I" is also not possible until you are fed up with the current master and open to noticing the real you, which has been patiently waiting for you to be done with the drama of the false self. Do you long for the goodness of your true nature? Do you long for God? Do you long to be done with the suffering caused by your judgments, mistaken beliefs, and negative feelings? Do you want peace and love more than you want your thoughts about yourself? Who or what would you be without your thoughts about you? Are you willing to discover this? The strength of your willingness and longing to be free of suffering and to know God will determine your readiness and ability to surrender.

Let's take a look at what is involved in surrendering the "I." Let's say that you find yourself caught up in a thought that makes you angry: "She shouldn't have done that to me!" Before you can surrender your (the false self's) anger, you first have to see that both the thought and the anger originated in the sense of "I."

The "I" has an idea about how people should and shouldn't behave. When someone doesn't comply with that belief, you feel angry. Did the person make you angry or did your belief? Your belief did. The "I" made the "I" angry. Do you want to feel angry? If not, the only way out is to surrender the belief that caused the anger. How do you do that? What is involved in surrendering a belief?

A belief is a thought, and a thought can only remain in existence if you give it attention. If you give a thought attention, you breathe life into it. Beliefs are thoughts that you have given so much attention to that you now firmly believe them. Without your attention, a thought cannot live for very long, and without your repeated attention, a thought cannot become a belief. You are very powerful! You animate and maintain the false self with your attention. You breathe life into the false self by giving your thoughts repeated attention. Without this attention, thoughts wither and beliefs fade away.

Furthermore, since you have to put your attention somewhere, when you withdraw it from a thought, your attention will breathe life into something else. What else might you enliven and sustain with your attention? If you put your attention on a flower, for instance, you will have the experience of the flower. If you hold your attention there long enough, you will feel a sense of merging with the flower and the joy that comes with that simple, yet profound experience.

What do you prefer: anger or the joy of fully experiencing a flower? You get to choose. Giving your attention fully to anything other than thoughts about yourself produces joy, peace, love and contentment. When you do that, you are no longer in the world of the false self but have entered the world of the true self, which is a world of unity with all life. You have moved from the prison of the ego to the Father's palace.

To the mind this sounds overly simplistic and not at all practical. And yet, giving attention to a flower or anything else that is real within your sensory environment is much more practical—functional—than giving attention to any thought you might have about you and your life, which at best serves no function at all and at worst serves a negative one.

"Blasphemy!" says the mind. "How dare you tamper with the cult of the mind, the cult of the *me*. How dare you attempt to break the spell of the false self!" That is exactly what happens every time you refuse to feed a thought about yourself or any other thought that maintains the false self, such as a fearful thought or an egoic desire. Fear is in place to keep you from leaving your egoic mind behind. That is fear's job, and it will not quiet down easily. So, you will have to surrender fear as well.

What power you have in attention! You create your experience of life with nothing more than your attention. Life allows you to create in this way. It allows you to have the experience you choose to create. You can have a life that is lost in the drama and pain of the false self or one that is an expression of the true self. It is your choice.

Surrendering the "I" and its beliefs is more of a not-doing than a doing. You cease doing what you normally and automatically do, which is feed a thought with your attention and more thoughts. Surrender feels like a sacrifice, a letting go of something you want, because people are naturally attached to doing what they have always done: think and believe their thoughts. Surrender is difficult because it feels like you have to give up something you love doing (thinking) for nothing, while quite the opposite is true.

The key to surrender is becoming aware of your *attachment* to a thought or feeling—to how much you want to be involved with it, even if that thought or feeling is not pleasant. Notice the pull that a thought or a feeling has on you and the sense of *needing* to be involved with it. In some cases, you may feel like you won't survive if you don't pay attention to a particular thought. This is especially the case when fear is involved.

When you are caught up in a thought or feeling, stop and take a few moments to let yourself explore and get to know the experience of that, including how a part of you enjoys feeling bad. The feeling of attachment is quite tangible, almost real. That is how convincing the mirage is. The attachment feels real, powerful, and difficult to let go of.

When you are under the influence of the attachment, it's got you. You are convinced that it is powerful and difficult to let go of. But when you just stop a moment and let yourself feel the attachment fully, something very interesting happens: The attachment loosens, and it is seen for what it is—a mirage, an illusion.

That which sees the illusion is not part of the illusion. It is the real self. When you choose to stop a moment and feel your attachment to a thought or feeling, what is able to do that is the real self. At that point, your real self has taken over and is being used to investigate the false self. The true captain is back on deck. Then you have a choice: You can go back to that train of thought or put your attention on something other than thoughts. The more you practice this, the easier it becomes to move beyond the egoic mind, the originator of the false self, and to know your true self.

Specifically, here are the steps involved in surrender. These steps are what you can do to *not* do what is conditioned and automatic, which is to get lost in thought:

1. Notice that you are caught up in a thought, a train of thoughts, or a feeling.

2. Gently tell yourself, "Stop." This breaks the egoic trance, the spell of the illusion. The pause provides an opportunity to make a choice between continuing to think or surrendering thinking.

3. During this pause, notice any attachment or desire to going back to that thought or feeling. It can help to mentally label it: "Attachment, desire to think." Feel free to name or describe it in whatever way makes the most sense to you.

4. Take a moment to feel that attachment in your body and more subtly energetically. Where is it located? In your gut? Heart? Head? Throat? Stomach? What does it feel like? Tight? Dark? Sticky? Grasping? Empty? Churning? Explore it. Examine it. Just be with the physical and energetic sense of it for a while with curiosity and interest.

5. Accept the attachment. Don't be upset about it or judge it. Being attached to thinking the thoughts that go through your mind is part of being human. There has never been a human who has not had such thoughts and been attached to them. As long as you are in a human body, it cannot be otherwise. But such attachments don't have to control where your attention goes. Once you are aware of being attached to a particular thought or feeling, you have a choice.

6. Next, broaden your awareness to include whatever else is present besides thoughts, feelings, and attachment to them. Look around you. Experience your environment through your senses. Notice what else is part of this moment in time. Is the sun shining? What sensations are you experiencing? What sounds do you hear? What are you aware of in your environment?

7. Now notice what is present on a more subtle level. The subtle level is the level in which the true self resides, and it is accessed by becoming aware of your sensory experience: Is love present? Peace? Relaxation? Awe? Compassion? A sense of beauty? Can you experience any of these even just a little? What is the experience like? Can you feel the aliveness that is the signature of your true self?

8. Give your attention more fully to the love, peace, joy, compassion, and acceptance of the true self, and you will come to know yourself as those qualities instead of as the false self. Over time, your ability to sense the subtle world of the true self will increase, and you will begin to live increasingly as your true self.

Surrender has a great reward, and that reward is love. When you surrender being lost in thought, you discover a new world, a subtle but more real world, which has been there all along, awaiting your notice and appreciation. You are what experiences this real world *and* you are everything you experience as well. That is the great mystery that is *you!*

Chapter 3

Surrendering Fear

The conditioned self, the false self, is run by fear and maintained by fear, which is the antithesis of love. Fear and love are at odds because fear distrusts and rejects life, while love trusts and embraces life. Therefore, fear and love cannot coexist. They represent points of view that do not intersect; either one or the other prevails.

Fear is the point of view of the ego, the primitive, conditioned aspect of yourself, which is largely what makes you human. Without an ego, people would readily experience their indwelling Spirit and the love it has for all life. With the ego, people experience fear, and because they do, they are driven to conquer, control, and dominate their environment and other human beings. The underlying belief driving the ego's behavior is "eat or be eaten." The ego's solution to the problem of survival is to conquer, be on top, vanquish. In pursuit of this, the ego seeks power, recognition, strength, beauty, and intelligence. If it attains these things, the ego believes that comfort, food, sex, safety, security, and happiness will be ensured.

Notice the absence of the word love in this description of the ego. There is no room for love in the ego's world unless love is seen as a means for achieving the ego's goals. Otherwise, love is presumed to be a potential weakness, a vulnerability. In love you let your guard down, you must trust someone not to hurt you, and you must share and compromise with another, all things that are abhorrent to the ego.

Until a person gains some mastery over the ego, his or her relationships are doomed to difficulty and dysfunction, because the ego is the enemy of love. The ego knows nothing about love, it does not value love, and it undermines and destroys love within oneself and in one's relationships.

Fear is what makes the ego what it is, and fear is what keeps someone from recognizing that he or she is something other than the false self. Until there is at least some recognition and involvement with the true self, there can be no happiness, for happiness and fear are mutually exclusive, just as love and fear are. True happiness comes from connection with one's true nature, with the love and peace at your core, not from getting or from dominating, which is the ego's strategy for happiness.

Because fear is so intimately tied to the ego, it is impossible to see past the ego until you have overcome fear to some degree. Those who have grown up in an unsafe or a threatening family or environment have great difficulty getting beyond their fear and, therefore, have difficulty relaxing into the love and peace of their true nature. They are forever on guard for the next attack, the next reproach.

While many live in such an environment today, most of you who are reading this do not live, at least any longer, in a punitive or unloving home or in a war zone. You are, for the most part, safe from immediate threats. And yet, even the safest and most comfortable of you suffers to some degree from various fears: fear of aging, ill health, poverty, loneliness, and death. Regardless of your situation in life, these are universal fears that must be dealt with.

I am here to help you surrender these universal fears, to help you trust, relax, and return to your true nature. I am here to deliver the message that not only do you have love and peace at your core, but so does the Intelligence behind all life: the Father. Do you believe this? If you did, how would this change how you feel and how you are in your life?

Take a moment, if you will, to take a deep breath and relax into the comfort of wherever you are. With each breath, allow yourself to sink more deeply into that comfort, that safety of whatever is holding you up. Allow yourself to feel how you are being supported by whatever is supporting you. Let yourself fully experience being held and supported. You are safe. You are here, and Life is supporting your existence here and now. In this moment, as in every moment, you are being taken care of.

It is a miracle, isn't it, how you arrived at this moment in time? And at every step of the way, in every moment, your existence was supported: by people, by opportunities, by things, by information, by guidance, by your own talents, by your intelligence, and by the magnificent miracle that is your body.

And in the next moment you will be supported and in the next, until you reach a time when your body no longer sustains you and you discover that you never needed your body to exist, as you continue to be nourished and supported in other dimensions—for eternity! There is no end to your existence, your power, your beauty. If you only knew how magnificent and powerful you are!

If you could more fully experience your eternal nature, you would easily embrace this life, which is so fleeting and so precious. From the standpoint of your true nature, this human experience is immeasurably valuable and treasured for the opportunities it provides for growth and for serving others.

You are going through whatever you are going through on this planet, in this dimension, for a reason—for many, many reasons, all of them purposeful, all of them worthwhile but which you may not understand. When you leave your mortal body, you continue to exist, and you take with you all the wisdom, knowledge, and talents you have acquired into the next adventure, the next stage of your existence.

From the standpoint of your soul, earth is the greatest of schools, like none other, and this lifetime is a grand and heroic undertaking. Your soul willingly embraces all manner of challenges you face here—all of them. Your soul has the strength and resources to benefit from every possible experience, regardless of how painful. And your soul has the power to heal every experience and be transformed by every experience.

If only you knew and could fully feel the excitement, enthusiasm, and joy that your soul feels for this gift of being alive now on earth. When you are able to step out of the ego's point of view, you can feel the love, wonderment, awe, and gratitude of your soul for this life. This is why it is so important to learn to move beyond the false self—because your life *can* be experienced as a blessing, as a precious gift.

It is possible even in this moment—right now—to feel this, simply by stopping to notice the love, joy, awe, and gratitude that are here right now. Are you willing to take a moment to do that? What might prevent you from doing that? Isn't it only a thought that would prevent this? Notice that thought, if it is there, and then turn away from it and turn your attention to the experience of this sweet moment. Stay with this experience long enough to feel the subtle happiness of your true self. Can you feel it, even just a little? The more you allow yourself to feel this, the more it becomes your reality.

This moment was designed just for you as a vehicle for experiencing the love that is within your heart. How else could God experience love as a human being unless God became one? How else could God experience such an adventure as this life without creating such a world as this? Can you feel God's pleasure in this, in His/Her creation, and the excitement of what might be discovered and learned from this unique place and moment in time?

Nowhere else in the universe is there a planet like this one. And nowhere else is there a person like you or circumstances like the ones you find yourself in. How quickly it all passes! From the standpoint of eternity, this life passes in the blink of an eye. One day, it will feel like that to you too. This lifetime will be but a vague memory, a story about someone you were long ago. Realizing how ephemeral and precious this life is will help you to cope with life's challenges, which are made much more difficult than they need to be by the ego.

Move out of the false self and discover the rich resources offered by your divine Self for overcoming and learning from your challenges. If you turn to the ego instead, you will get stuck in suffering. But something else knows the way out of all suffering. This mysterious something is your salvation, your means for happiness and peace. But you must turn to it, choose it, get to know it, and learn to live from it. It is who you really are. You know when you have found it because it feels like arriving home. You know it by the love you feel in your heart and by the "peace that passeth all understanding."

When you feel this love and peace, know that you have found your way Home and that this is how life is meant to feel. You are not meant to suffer, except when you are aligned with the ego and believing the ego's perceptions. Suffering is how you are shown what is false, what *not* to believe, what *not* to trust. You can trust your suffering to show you what is false in this world, and you can trust love and peace to show you what is true and trustworthy.

Always go in the direction of love, and you cannot go wrong. This is the simple compass you have been given to point you Homeward. As long as you listen to your thoughts, it will be difficult to find your way. You will suffer and be confused. But when you stop listening to your thoughts, you will find freedom, peace, and happiness, and your heart will be full of love, gratitude, and awe.

Fear is the great hurdle. Fear keeps you in your suffering. Fear keeps you believing what your thoughts tell you about yourself, about others, about life—all lies, or nearly so. When you look, you discover that so little in your thoughts is true and helpful, so little, in fact, that you will never miss your thoughts about yourself and your life. They have never helped you find your way but only caused you to lose your way.

But how can I convince the fearful mind? You must convince yourself by seeing for yourself the truth of what I am saying. Look at what you are thinking. Are your thoughts true, helpful, and wise? Or are they confused, unkind, petty, and largely untrue? Don't your thoughts argue both sides of an issue? One day you are on one side of an issue or a choice, and the next day you are on the other side. Following the voice in your head is like riding in a boat without a rudder: It moves forward but with no clear direction, or it spins around in circles.

All the while, the mind is full of judgment, anger, complaints, and pettiness, rarely happy, rarely content. There is no peace, no relaxation, no gratitude, no contentment, no love when you listen to your thoughts. They never let you rest: You are never good enough. Life is never good enough. Others are never good enough.

Feel the tension and contraction in your body when you think your thoughts. That tells you something about them. That contraction is a form of suffering. It is a sign of disconnection from your source and a sign that you need to align with something truer and more real than the voice in your head.

What else is here? How do you experience the still, small voice within? How can you experience your sweet Self? You experience it by saying no to that which takes you away from it, by saying no to your thoughts, particularly to your thoughts of fear. And then you listen for that still, small voice, patiently. You make room for it, you wait for it, and you allow it to be heard.

Your fears are fantasies or, more accurately, nightmarish illusions. Your mind makes your fears up, and then the feelings they create in your body convince you that your fears are real—but they are not! They are imaginations rather than what is or what will be. Your fears are no more true or real than the monsters in novels or movies. Your fears are created by your ego to keep you listening to it. That is all they are. That is their sole purpose.

It may be that the things you fear have happened to someone at some time in the universe. But to assume that what you fear will happen to you is a leap of faith—faith in a fantasy. If only you had as much faith in the truth, which is that you have the inner resources for dealing with your challenges and that every challenge serves a purpose in your growth. Furthermore, every challenge has a gift to offer, and how much you suffer in the face of a challenge depends on how much you listen to your thoughts.

Some of the most compelling fears are fears of poverty, illness, pain, disability, and death. It is natural to be afraid of these things. The mind is programmed to contemplate worst-case scenarios. However, doing this is not as functional as it may seem. Having these fears and examining such possibilities does not prevent or protect you from experiencing what you fear. Being afraid of something also doesn't cause it to happen. There is no magic in fearful thoughts. A fearful thought has nothing to do with what actually happens and doesn't actually help you cope with whatever does happen.

Do you see that such fears do not arise as a prediction or forewarning of an actual event? You have had many, many fears in your lifetime, and they have not manifested. Fearful thoughts arise regularly, spontaneously, and randomly, often without a connection to anything real.

When fearful thoughts are connected to an event, such as a toothache or job loss, the mind tends to pile on more fearful thoughts, which increase the fear and other unpleasant emotions. Without the fear and confusion of the egoic mind, what are you left with in the face of a toothache, a job loss, a diagnosis, or some other difficulty? You are left with this moment, which is all you ever have. You always have only this moment and this moment's experience. And that is where the solution to your so-called problems lies.

If some pain or other problem is calling for your attention, then you do what you can about it. You take steps. If this is not a moment for taking steps, then leave all thoughts about the problem alone. Do not pick those thoughts up and run with them. Do not think about what might happen, what the problem might mean, or how it might affect you. Do you see how useless these types of thoughts are? They do not lead to answers and they don't change a thing.

Even thinking about what to do about a problem is not where the solution lies. The mind will spin around in circles, trying to figure out what to do, but the best answers come from deep inside: At a certain point, you just *know* what to do or you find yourself inspired to take a particular action.

Your true self will take care of you if you give it a chance to. But you must listen to something other than your thoughts. You must listen to the communications of the true self, which are subtler than the thoughts in your head. The true self communicates through intuition, knowings, inspiration, and urges to act. Unfortunately, the thoughts set in motion by the fearful thoughts produce additional emotions and exhaustion, making it more difficult to function and tune in to the true self's subtle communications.

This over-involvement with the mind and emotions leaves people feeling hopeless, powerless, and bad about their life. The false self takes an experience, like an illness or a job loss, and puts itself at the center of a story about it: "This always happens to me. Just when I was doing so well. Now this. I can never get on top of things." Such storytelling about one's life only magnifies the fear, unhappiness, and pain. It causes unnecessary suffering.

Why would you want to increase your pain this way? I am sure you don't, and you don't have to once you are aware of how the egoic mind creates suffering whenever something happens that it doesn't like: "My life is not supposed to go this way! Life is unfair. I never get what I want." That kind of thinking never serves. Life goes as it goes, and everyone must learn to take whatever life brings in stride, which is to say, accept things the way they are and not take them personally.

To enter the Father's palace, you must surrender to your life as it is. You must surrender "your life," that is, the story of your life. And you must surrender your fears about what may be. You must leave them behind. There is no need for such fears where you are going (Home, to the present moment). You never needed your fears anyway, which is what you discover if you can trust enough to move beyond them.

The key to overcoming your fearful thoughts is staying in the present moment. Fearful thoughts are by nature thoughts about the future—a possible frightening future. This future doesn't and never will exist, although the mind makes such thoughts seem real and important. They are an illusion. The only thing that is real is your present moment experience, the experience you are having right *now*.

Under even the most difficult circumstances, if you are able to be in the here and now rather than in your thoughts *about* it and take life one moment at a time, you will discover that you have the resources for dealing with any challenge.

When people get caught up in their thoughts and feelings, they lose access to their inner resources. Fear activates the body's fight-or-flight response, which deactivates the part of the brain that helps you reason and tap in to your intuition. So, being caught in thoughts and feelings of fear is more of an immobilizing state than a helpful one.

To access the part of your brain that you need for overcoming challenges, your rational mind and your inner wisdom, you need to surrender your thoughts and fears and become very present in the here and now. When you do that, the physiological effects of fear disappear, and you are capable of taking wise action, if action is needed.

Turning your attention to what you are experiencing here and now, in the present moment, vanquishes all fear. From this place, it is easy to see your life more clearly, from the perspective of the true self. When you stay in the here and now, not only do you gain access to wisdom and right action, but you also realize you are eternal and being supported by a loving universe in which you are deeply cared for. You feel grateful for existing in this moment and curious and interested in what may happen next.

The state of mind, or consciousness, that is the true self is as different from the state of mind of the false self as night is to day. It is like waking up from a nightmare into a beautiful, loving, caring world. Fear creates the nightmare and sustains it. Seeing that fear is an illusion and serves no positive purpose frees you from having to experience the nightmare caused by unnecessary fear.

What you discover is that you never needed any thoughts about the future, because the future takes care of itself when you allow yourself to be fully present in the here and now, where you really exist. The false self exists in the past and future, as an idea of yourself, but the true self inhabits the present—alone, for the false self cannot exist in the present moment. The false self dissolves as soon as you land in the present moment. Then all that exists is the wonderment, awe, beauty, love, peace, and joy of your true self.

Because people rarely stay in the present moment for long before their thoughts catch them up once again, this description of the present moment may sound unrealistic and unattainable. But it is not. Everyone is destined to discover the power of the present moment and that of their true self.

Surrendering fear is key in this discovery, as fear is the monster at the gate that leads to the Father's palace. But the monster is an illusion! Fortunately, you don't even have to fight with an illusion to overcome it. All you need to do is realize that it is an illusion. Fear is an illusion! Are you willing to trust this? Surrendering fear requires trusting that the monsters of the mind are illusions and then being willing to walk past them and enter the palace of the present moment.

Many a hero in myths and legends has been in this position. The hero sends out a call or prayer for help in getting past the monster at the gate, after which aid appears in some form, possibly simply as an idea or inspiration to do something. When you are faced with a fear that you are convinced is true, send out a call or prayer for help and know that it will be answered. The hero always succeeds, but never solely by virtue of his own strength, but with the help of the gods. Do ask, and you shall receive. Know this. It is a law of life.

Ask for help and then surrender your fear to the Father. Put it in His hands, give it to Him, and let it be His "problem." So often, it is feelings of powerlessness and hopelessness that keep people stuck in their thoughts and fears. Surrender these feelings too to the Father, put them at His feet, in His hands, and let Him take care of what seems too big or difficult for you to handle by yourself. You see, you are never alone, unless you choose to be.

Each person has the strength of the universe behind him or her, if you but ask for it.

Chapter 4

Surrendering "I Want"

One of the most compelling "I" thoughts is the thought "I want." People love to think about what they want. Their desires are food for fantasies about their future life, as if all you had to do was mentally design a future life and then step into it and live it. This is how the ego seems to believe life is shaped or *should* be shaped, without acknowledging that something else much more powerful, which trumps the personal will, is shaping life alongside the ego's desires.

One's desires are not as powerful as the ego supposes or wishes them to be, and this is the cause of much unhappiness, dissatisfaction, and anger. If you agree with the ego's perception that life should comply or you should be able to get it to comply with your desires, you will be sorely disappointed, for although life sometimes does do this, it often does not, no matter how strongly you desire something or how much you apply yourself to getting it. There is no magic formula for getting what you want because there is a larger force, a greater will, that ultimately determines whether you do or not.

This is not good news to the ego. Its desires are extremely important to it. Getting what it wants is the ego's strategy for survival, for keeping safe and finding some security in this "perilous" world. The ego is afraid of the world, so it sets out to get certain things for itself to ensure its safety and happiness.

Who can blame it? When the world is seen through the ego's eyes, this makes perfect sense. The problem is that the world is not as the ego perceives it to be, and so the ego's strategy is flawed. A strategy that is based on misperceptions or only part of the truth is bound to not be very useful and may, in fact, lead to poor results. And so it does.

Trying to create a life as you imagine it when life is not designed to give you that can only lead to frustration and unhappiness. Life has its own design and reason for being, and that reason is not to give your ego what it wants, although the ego does sometimes get what it wants.

The ego is not meant to be the master creator of your life. It is the aspect of the human being that creates conflict, complications, confusion, unpleasant emotions, and bad karma. How can something like that create a beautiful and fulfilling life? And yet, that is what is at the helm of most people's lives.

No wonder there is so much suffering and unhappiness in this world: At the helm is a rather diabolical aspect of the human being, not the divine aspect. The ego is the villain in the human drama. Fortunately, the Divine is ultimately what is in control of life, not the ego. The Divine allows the ego to have some control because this leads to lessons and consequently to growth, which is part of the divine design.

The ego's desires, then, are misguided, because what is behind such desires is not wise enough to know what is best for oneself, only what is assumed to be best based on the ego's misunderstandings about life and about what makes for happiness.

The problem is that the ego's perceptions are skewed by fear. Every fear the false self has becomes a desire:

The false self fears powerlessness, so it desires power over others, not realizing that real power comes from uniting with others, not subordinating them.

The false self fears poverty, so it desires wealth, not realizing that real wealth comes from love and loving relationships.

The false self fears obscurity, so it desires recognition, not realizing that all the recognition in the world will not make it feel seen or erase the sense of lack it feels.

The false self fears death, so it desires to live on in monuments, not realizing that it never did exist and that what is real is eternal.

The false self fears aging, so it desires the fountain of youth, not realizing that it is not the body.

The false self fears not knowing, so it desires knowledge, not realizing that knowledge without wisdom is folly.

The false self fears imprisonment, so it desires to imprison those it perceives as enemies, not realizing that the real enemy is within.

The false self fears dependence, so it desires individuality and separation, not realizing that Oneness and interdependence is the nature of life and the individual's own salvation.

The false self fears being unloved and alone, so it desires love from others, not realizing that love is not something you get from others, but what you experience when you give love to others.

The false self is not wise enough to recognize these truths. It knows nothing of truth, only the opposite of truth. The false self is the purveyor of untruth. That is what it is. It is, after all, the *false* self and named that for a reason. It is not only an imposter and unreal, but its perceptions are false and its desires therefore misguided.

This is not to say there is anything wrong with the ego's desires. It is natural to have an ego and to have such desires. There is also nothing wrong with pursuing these desires. Doing so provides experiences and the many lessons that come with having those experiences, and ultimately the truth about egoic desires is discovered. It just would be a mistake to assume that getting what the ego wants is the purpose of your life or of life in general. That is much too shortsighted a view and overlooks a much grander purpose.

What is that purpose? The overarching purpose is to return to the Father by reclaiming your sonship, by recognizing your own inner divinity. Aside from that, each of you has a purpose for choosing to be on earth at this time in your particular body-mind. You came here for a reason. That reason is for the most part unknown to you, as it is meant to be, for your purpose is, in a sense, to discover your purpose, which happens in the course of living your life.

Life reveals your purpose to you in a variety of ways. It brings you certain experiences, people, and opportunities, and it closes the door on others. The Father has a design for your life, and it is unveiled little by little, moment by moment. The design unfolds each day as it is meant to.

In the midst of this unfolding design, you make choices about the life that is being given to you. You choose the specifics and you choose your attitude and responses, but you do not choose the stage upon which your life is set. Although your life is by no means scripted or predetermined, it is circumscribed, steered, shaped, and sometimes determined by particular events that you are meant to experience.

A higher plan is in effect in people's lives, whether they are aware of that or not. To the extent that they are aware of that plan or are willing to see that there is one, they are more likely to align with it and be fulfilled by it. On the other hand, to the extent that they see the purpose of their life as getting what they want and they judge the value and rightness of their life by how successfully they manage to do that, they will suffer.

Although you have been given free will for a reason, life is not here to support your personal will, but to fulfill a greater plan in which your individual will plays only a small part. The more your individual will is aligned with the higher will, the happier you will be. When your will is identical to Thy will, you thrive and find the deepest contentment and peace.

You know that you are aligned with Thy will when you feel the peace, contentment, joy, and love of your inner divinity. This is what I am calling the Son, or the true self. The Father *in you* is the Son. The Son knows the way, while the false self does not. The false self doesn't even recognize that there is a way, much less know the way. But the Son does. This divine spark is given to you so that you don't lose your way in life, so that you will fulfill your destiny, your designated purpose.

What I am saying about life is not a religious fairytale, told to appease you within a sorrowful and hopelessly desolate world, but the absolute truth about life. Too many have discarded the truth hidden in religious teachings because they could not accept other aspects of those teachings. But the truth about life is beyond any belief system or religion and can be readily observed and experienced easily enough for those who have eyes to see.

The truth is that your life is divinely designed and divinely guided moment to moment by loving forces whose sole purpose is to serve you. Many of you are able to feel or even communicate with these forces, so for you, this truth is self-evident. But for those who are not aware of their presence, the first step is to *believe* that these guiding forces exist. Once you believe this, you will begin to experience their presence. Belief in their existence opens the door for greater awareness of them and for receiving even more assistance from them.

What you believe determines what you experience. This is how that works: Spiritual forces respect your free will, so they allow you to make choices and experience the results of those choices. If you choose to believe that nothing exists beyond the physical, then you won't notice anything more subtle than your five senses. Even if, on occasion, you do notice something, you will discount and overlook it, thereby reinforcing your belief that spiritual forces don't exist. On the other hand, if you believe that spiritual forces exist, then that belief invites them to more actively assist you. Because you believe you are being guided, you are likely to notice instances when that is the case, thereby confirming your belief—and the truth.

Guiding forces do assist you to some extent even if you do not believe in them because such forces are intrinsic and essential to human evolution. However, they will participate in your life much more fully if you invite them to. That participation can only be beneficial because their nature is goodness and their purpose is to serve humankind. It is not within them to harm or mislead you. The closer you are to these loving forces, the more they are able to protect you from those whose intentions are to interfere with your happiness and life plan, since such forces do exist as well.

The knowledge that life is this benevolent can't help but open your heart. Those who have a connection with other dimensions and levels of their being naturally feel love: for life, for God, for creation, call it what you will. When you are in touch with the truth about life, you feel happy, loving, and at peace. Feeling this way is your birthright! This is how you are meant to feel and how you *can* feel.

Love is the natural outcome of knowing the truth and not being taken in by the fear and lies of the false self. When you surrender the false self, you fall into the truth, into the love that is behind all creation, which happens to also be within *you*. The greatest fulfillment is feeling this love, because love is the greatest truth about life. Love is God, the force behind creation, your very being, and what upholds your very existence. Love created all that is and love is what sustains it.

Two thousand years ago, I came to redeem the world through love: to right any misunderstandings, teach love, and proclaim the truth, which is that this is a loving universe and each of you is the beloved Son of a caring and forgiving Father.

Punishment and vengefulness have never been the intent behind any difficulty you experience. God is love and has nothing but love for creation. Within creation is free will, and the gift of free will is sometimes a curse, as you are free to choose to believe thoughts that cause you to suffer, limit yourself, and harm others. That you choose to believe those thoughts is not the intent of God, but chosen freely by you.

You could argue that God created the ego and therefore suffering, but you would be forgetting that *you* are God incarnate as the Son, that you, as God and through your soul, willingly chose to become human and to experience all that comes with that, including having an ego.

Because people have forgotten that they have chosen this, at times they feel victimized by the hardships of this world and by the emotions, conflict, and problems created by their own egos. They blame God for their pain without realizing that most of it is self-generated and perpetuated by an ego that does not know how to love.

God challenges Himself/Herself by creating a world such as yours with both a positive and negative pole. This means that there are beings who are oriented toward love (the positive pole) and those who are oriented toward fear and power (the negative pole, or the opposite of love).

Beings who are oriented toward fear and power or who themselves have an ego are responsible for creating and sustaining the ego in humanity. And God allows that to be as it is. God allows for His/Her creations to create in ways that might cause suffering, all the while knowing that this will result in learning and better choices. Eventually, everyone relinquishes the negative pole and returns home to Love.

Having an ego makes it possible to experience negativity and, by contrast, to appreciate the positive pole: love. Moreover, the negative pole brings experiences that you/God would never otherwise have and growth that you/God would never otherwise have. Yes, God grows or, more accurately, God's creations grow and evolve, and God is enriched by that.

To return to the subject of surrender, it may be necessary to surrender at least some of your ego's desires at the feet of Thy will. Surrendering all of these desires is never necessary, only the ones that might interfere with the accomplishment of Thy will. If you are unwilling to surrender those or if you are unaware of the need to surrender them, then you are likely to suffer, as Thy will, will be done. The conflict between the small will and the greater will and the unwillingness to surrender the small will to divine will is one of the primary causes of human suffering.

The ego is sure that what it wants is what it needs, and that misunderstanding causes so much suffering. Attachment to what the ego wants is strengthened by the belief that those desires are important and meaningful, when they aren't.

You cannot name an egoic desire that is actually important and meaningful. Any desire that is important and meaningful does not come from the ego but from your divinity, your true self. That is how you know whether a desire is important or not: Where does it come from?

It is possible to tell where a desire comes from by paying close attention to the experience of that desire. Take the desire "I want more money." When you let yourself experience wanting more money, what does that feel like in your body and energy? It feels tight and contracted, right? Now, let yourself feel the desire "I want more love." Even that feels contracted. The problem is "I want."

Anything that follows those two words, "I want," is bound to create a sense of contraction, even "I want love, peace, and joy." Even higher desires such as these feel contracted when expressed as a thought with "I" as the subject. This is because they are being expressed by the "I," or false self, which inherently feels empty and lacking.

The false self wants something because it perceives itself as not having it, as lacking it and therefore needing it. The truth, however, is that you do not lack anything you need, especially love, peace, and joy, because these are qualities of your essential nature and cannot *not* be already here.

It is impossible to lack love, peace, or joy, so "I want more love, peace, and joy" is a statement that is not aligned with the reality that love, peace, and joy are already here. When you think or believe something that is not aligned with reality, you feel contracted, and rightfully so! The contraction or tension in your body lets you know that what you are thinking is not true.

An important and meaningful desire, on the other hand, is simply *felt*. You might put that desire into words, but it doesn't initially appear as a thought. As soon as you put it into words, those words make you feel as if something is missing. If you don't put it into words but just feel that desire and allow it to move you as it will, then you will be expressing divine will.

Thy will is not experienced as the thought "I want," but as a feeling, urge, inspiration, or drive that moves you in a particular direction. Everyone has felt this and does feel this many times a day. You are naturally moved throughout your day by something that is alive in you and motivating you to sustain yourself and unfold your life plan. This mysterious something is Thy will, as expressed through the Son, the Divine in you.

This means that if you surrender "I want," you won't lose anything but a sense of lack and a possible misdirection of your energy. In its place, something else arises, which moves you to take actions or take a rest, as necessary. You can trust this inner force to live your life. It is all that ever has lived your life, although this innate motivation so often gets coopted by the ego.

The more you let go of "I want," the more you make room for something else to move you, and that something is very wise, very kind, and knows exactly what you need to be happy and fulfilled. What it wants *is* really what you need. This motivating force is love.

Chapter 5

Surrendering Knowing

Surrendering knowing is not about surrendering actual knowledge but surrendering untruths and the pretense of actual knowledge. What makes this especially challenging is that people often don't realize they are holding onto untruths or pretending to know. The egoic mind is very tricky!

Built into your thoughts is the sense that they are true, so why would you question them? That is the problem. People generally don't question their thoughts because they assume their thoughts are true or, at the very least, that those thoughts are their own real opinions about life and, therefore, valuable and at least personally true.

Knowledge is a good thing. No one would argue that. Knowing how to get from your home to where you work is essential. Knowing what day it is, what words to use to describe things, how to read, how to do math, how to test a hypothesis—this knowledge is necessary and extremely useful.

The part of your brain that learns, retains knowledge, and evaluates and applies knowledge is exactly what is needed to see that the thoughts that come into your mind do not pass the intelligence test. You have a mind that learns and processes knowledge, and you have the thoughts that come into your mind—the egoic mind. These are two very different kinds of thinking: one is intelligent and the other is essentially programming.

If you had a computerized voice that was programmed with some information, rules, and general advice, you would have something close to the egoic mind, with one very important difference: The egoic mind is petty, unkind, judgmental, bossy, critical, and generally dissatisfied. If this does not describe your egoic mind, then you are one of the few fortunate souls who was gifted with a computerized inner voice that is not also a complainer.

Progress along the spiritual path often neutralizes some of the negativity of one's thoughts, but rarely does the egoic mind disappear completely. In all likelihood, the voice in your head is there to stay and must be dealt with.

The first step in dealing with the egoic mind is getting to know it: What are the thoughts that run through your mind? What are the most common ones? Write them down. That way, you can examine them more objectively.

The second step is to do just that—question your thoughts: Are they true? Are they useful? Do you need them? How do they affect you? Do you like how you are being affected by them? If not, what can you do about that?

The third step is to see that you have some power in relation to your thoughts. They are, after all, yours, so you can do with them what you choose. You can believe them and act on them *or not.* You can evaluate the possible consequences of acting on them before you do and choose otherwise if you don't want those consequences.

Life is a great mystery and so are human beings. There are many more questions than answers. You can know lots of things and lots of facts and still not know what life is all about, what your life is about, why things are the way they are, what's going to happen, why people behave the way they do or did, why things happened the way they did, and on and on. There are many more things that you don't know and never will know than you do. It's important to realize and admit this.

This is where the false self falls down: It does not admit what it doesn't know. Instead, it pretends to know things that can never be known as well as things that may be known at some point but aren't known yet. If you met someone who did this, you would call that person a pathological liar, which is someone who makes up things that aren't true and tries to pass them off on others as if they were true. That is a description of your egoic mind.

Do you need these thoughts? This is a very good question. Take a look and answer this for yourself. You certainly don't need any thoughts that don't actually have the answer to something but pretend to. Spotting such thoughts isn't actually that hard. You just have to stop a moment and ask yourself, "Do I really know that?" You may be quite surprised at how often the answer is no.

This is how you discover the truth about your thoughts. You have to ask yourself some questions. They are very simple questions, but ones that most people don't ever think to ask themselves. If you even suggest to others that they question their thoughts, most will look at you funny, as if there's something wrong with you.

The programming does not want to be questioned. It is not meant to be uncovered. And yet the truth eventually comes out at some point in a person's evolution. It is time now in humanity's evolution for the truth to come out, which is why there are more and more teachings like this one being made available.

The world can no longer withstand the ego's domination. The ego must be made subordinate, and love must take its place. But because you have free will, you have to do the work yourself of seeing this and freeing yourself from your own ego. Those of us assisting humanity in this transformation can only point out the truth.

Here are some common examples of the mind pretending to know when it doesn't:

> *You think you know what someone thinks about you.*
>
> *You think you know how someone feels about you.*
>
> *You think you know how someone feels about something.*
>
> *You think you know why something happened or why someone did what he or she did.*
>
> *You think you know what someone else is going to do.*
>
> *You think you know what you are going to do.*
>
> *You think you know what someone else should do.*
>
> *You think you know what you should do.*
>
> *You think you know what will make someone happy.*
>
> *You think you know what will make you happy.*
>
> *You think you will like or not like someone (as if you ever feel just one way about someone).*
>
> *You think you know how some experience will feel.*
>
> *You think you know how you will feel in the future.*
>
> *You think you know what's going to happen in the world.*
>
> *You think you know what is happening in the world.*
>
> *You think you know the solution to what's happening in the world.*
>
> *You think you know what your life is going to look like tomorrow.*
>
> *You think you know what you are going to do tomorrow.*
>
> *You think you know what you are going to do in the next few hours.*

You think...

"I think..." Watch those two words, please, as they point to speculation on the part of the mind, a mere idea that is often based on very little information or knowledge. Often such thoughts have no basis in reality whatsoever. The mind just likes to think, so it thinks thoughts. It comes up with ideas pretty much out of the blue. Notice how much of your conversations with others are based on opinions and theories about anything and everything.

This is what the mind does. It produces thoughts, opinions, judgments, and evaluations, among other things. These are not the objective evaluations and conclusions that your rational mind is capable of, but a horse of a completely different color. This is not intelligence functioning, but programming. Pure and simple. Watch the mind. See for yourself.

Seeing the truth can be quite humbling—and extremely freeing. You become free of the need to have an opinion about everything, to know about all of the things that you never could know about anyway. What a relief it is to not have to know everything! And to not *need* to know. The false self feels a need to know everything, even when it can't, while the true self simply knows what it needs to know when it needs to know it, without desiring anything more than that.

Another benefit of disengaging from the mind's pretend knowings is that your mental energy is freed up for other activities, perhaps for learning or for some other practical or fun application of the mind. Since you can only be involved in one kind of mental activity at a time, what will it be: the idle speculation of the egoic mind, including all the thoughts about yourself, or more intellectual pursuits such as questioning your thoughts, investigating the subtle realms, reading, learning, or creating something?

One of the most wonderful gifts you have been given is a mind that can explore, imagine, create, and learn. The being that you are is naturally curious and fascinated by life and loves to learn. Such enjoyable mental activities can replace the useless ruminations, fantasies, and speculations of the mind.

When you are spending less time mentally spinning your wheels and dealing with the emotions generated by that, you will have more time for more fun, fulfilling, and meaningful activities, including just being. Furthermore, a quieter mind means you will be able to tune in to the spiritual Heart and its guidance more easily.

When you stop listening to the mind and begin listening more deeply to something much subtler than the mind, your life will change. Then it will be possible for you to see how truly good life is, how supportive and trustworthy it is. Your thoughts were what was creating any harshness, anxiety, fear, distrust, stress, and dissatisfaction you felt. Once you stop creating a negative internal climate by listening to your thoughts, then all that is left is love, wonder, awe, gratitude and joy—the truth about life. When life is stripped of the ego's perceptions and emotions and experienced through different eyes, life is seen more truly. Love is all around for those who have eyes to see it.

When you see from the eyes of love, you see love. When you see from the ego's eyes, you see life as the ego sees it. Whatever lens you look from is what you see and what you experience. If you want to change your life, change the lens through which you look. All real change and transformation is the result of such a change of lens.

All that has ever kept you from your true self are your false ideas. These ideas are everything you think you know about yourself and everything else. With every false idea that you surrender, you are transformed, and the lens through which you look becomes clearer. In this way, you become who you are meant to be: your true self.

The process of becoming clearer—or empty, as the Buddhists say—is to recognize how much you do not know, notice how attached your ego is to pretending to know, and offer this attachment and all misunderstandings and false ideas to the Father. Give them to Him. Lay them at His feet. Imagining yourself doing this is a very powerful act of clearing. This act strengthens your intention to become free of such useless thoughts and calls forth spiritual forces to help you with this.

To enter the Father's palace, you have to surrender your attachment to knowing, not to real knowledge, but attachment to the ego's false beliefs and assumptions, which create and maintain the false self. To surrender this, you have to be willing to not know, which the ego is not. What *is* willing to not know is the true self.

This surrender may seem difficult, but all it takes is a *willingness* to surrender and a *willingness* to not know. This willingness will naturally take you to surrender. Your intention is powerful! It is an important ingredient in the process of surrendering the false self. You don't need to know how to surrender; you only need to be willing to, and the *how* is taken care of.

Are you willing? Are you willing to be stripped bare of all thoughts about yourself, the past, the future, what you think you know, and what you'd like to know? What would that be like? Who would you be? You would lose a lot of what seems to make you who you are, but you would not be losing anything that is real, and what you would gain is your true self.

How can I describe your true self to you? There are no words, but it is closer to you than your breath. The true self is known only through experience, and the more experiences you have of it, the deeper those experiences become and the more real the reality of the true self becomes. There is no end to the depths of this self. Are you willing to experience it and stay in that experience for as long as it takes to get to know your true self? Now, that is true knowing!

Stop a moment and feel what it is like to be in this moment, stripped of all knowing. What remains? What is that? Consciousness? Existence? You exist. You are conscious. You exist *as* consciousness, and that is all! That is all you really know. In not needing to know anything more than that, lies peace. You have come Home. You can just be. Finally, there is no need to grasp after more, to know more. What you know is enough. Existence is enough.

And then... you find yourself being moved by some knowing that arises from deep within you. Without warning or knowing why, suddenly you feel called to act, and you answer that call. You don't need to know anything more. Answering that call is natural, spontaneous, and automatic, except sometimes you stop yourself—your thoughts stop you.

The call sometimes comes in the form of an idea that pops into your mind, but it is unlike the usual thoughts. It has been described as a light bulb going on or an "aha!" because that is what an idea from the Father feels like. It feels expansive, good, and true. When the call lands in the body, it is often described as an intuition or a download.

You are given instructions for this life, which are delivered little by little, moment to moment, as you need them. These instructions are usually very sparse; nothing is given that you don't immediately need. They are more like pointers or clues for you to follow in your own way.

These pointers are very different from the mind's instructions, which are spelled out specifically and handed out continually. If only those thoughts were wise! But the Father wants *you*, the Son, the unique and beloved individual that He created and infused with His spirit, to choose the specifics, not your ego. The Father gave you free will so that you could fill in the specifics as you will. The Father guides you only generally and then steps back to enjoy what you choose to create *with* Him.

The Father's instructions do not feel at all like the demands and to-do lists of the egoic mind but more like reminders, nudges, encouragement, inspiration, motivation, and excitement about doing something or taking on something. In that way, they are not like instructions at all. They offer no long-term plan or reasons why or details, except what you might receive moment to moment, and there is no requirement that you fulfill these instructions, although doing so feels right and brings you joy.

The Father's instructions are a gift, an ongoing guiding Presence that is designed to take care of you, make you happy, and fulfill you in this lifetime. You can trust the knowings from your spiritual Heart to do that. They are what unfolds life and always has, alongside the dictates of your mind.

Now that you know that you need only the Father's instructions, you can disregard the voice in your head, the imposter who poses as the captain. You never needed that voice, but you had to discover that for yourself. And you have had to discover for yourself that still, small voice. And now, moment to moment, it is up to you to choose that quiet, unimposing voice over the ego's noisy, imperious one.

There has always been a plan, and you have always been guided to fulfill it through that still, small voice. That voice is rarely a voice, and yet everyone knows what is meant when it is described this way, because it is closer to you than anything else. It is, in essence, your own voice calling you Home.

Chapter 6

Surrendering to Love in Relationships

I have been speaking about surrendering thoughts in exchange for experiencing the love that is your true nature. This chapter will explore what it means to share this love with others through relationship. It is one thing to drop into the unconditional love of your true nature and quite another to be able to bring that love into your relationships, where one is so often challenged by another's conditioning and ego as well as one's own.

What I mean by conditioning is the preferences, personality traits, beliefs, images, fantasies, desires, fears, psychological issues, and habit patterns that cause people to behave reflexively and automatically in the ways they generally do. The false self is the sum total of this conditioning plus the ego. The true self is what you are beyond the ego and all of this conditioning, and it is what is capable of love.

Conditioning is responsible for all the ways people are different from each other. In addition to the ego, these differences are what cause problems in relationships. In any of your relationships, you are going to have to relate to the other person's ego and conditioning, and that's where relationships run into trouble. The true selves don't have a problem with each other; after all, they are in essence the same!

Because most people relate to other people's egos and conditioning from their own ego and conditioning, most relationships are an experience of one ego relating to another and one set of conditioning battling with another. On that level, love doesn't stand a chance. Egos want to get their way and be right more than they want love. They will fight to the death of the relationship, and often do.

The only chance that love has is if two people are able to experience their own true self and that of the other at least some of the time. Fortunately, experiencing your true self is not only *not* impossible, but inevitable if love is given half a chance. The true self in each person *is* love and lives for love, so the true selves of each are always pulling the person toward love. Love is a very powerful force in people's lives, and the drive for love motivates people to keep trying to find the love that they know in their heart is possible. Love is possible, and something inside you knows this and, against all odds (the ego), keeps trying to get it right.

The ego is the enemy of love. It fears love, although it needs other people's love to feel good about itself and to feel safe. And yet, relationships feel quite unsafe and challenging to the ego because of its lack of control over the other person and the potential hurt involved in relationships. Love presents quite a dilemma to the ego!

Because the ego is incompatible with love, a relationship will be only as strong and loving as both people's ability to surrender their own egos. The surrender I am talking about is not a sacrificing, or subjugation, of one person in deference to the other's needs and ego, which often happens in relationship, but the recognition by both that mutual happiness is possible only when both are willing to put love and the relationship first and sort out their differences from that vantage point. *Both* must be willing to surrender their egos and conditioning for a higher cause—for love and for the relationship.

In the face of a conflict, which is inevitably about differences in conditioning, often one person has to surrender his or her ego's position first before the other person will. As in a war, when one side puts down its weapons, the other side will too. Once that is done, peace—love—is possible, and a mutually agreed upon solution to those differences can be found from the vantage point of the true selves.

Most of the time, however, the battle around conditioning is a personal one and is best if it remains a personal one. What I mean by this is that the battle is *within* you and doesn't have to involve the other person. It is your personal battle with your own conditioning and ego, which demands that your partner be more like you or comply with your likes, dislikes, expectations, fantasies, and desires. The conditioning itself isn't necessarily a problem, but your ego makes it a problem by demanding that others change to please you, to meet your needs, to match your expectations, desires, fantasies, and images.

Your conditioning doesn't have to become a problem for the relationship. If you don't like something about your partner, is that your problem, your partner's problem, or both? Most of the time, it is simply your problem, but you make it your partner's problem and, consequently, something the relationship has to deal with. *Your* problem—some unmet expectation or desire or your dislike of something—becomes a problem in the relationship.

Many issues could be solved quite easily if people simply recognized the difference between their personal issue with someone and a real problem that needs the other person's attention. Most problems in relationship are caused simply by one person not liking something about the other: one person's conditioning bumping up against the other's. This is always going to happen. There will always be differences.

The solution is not to try to eliminate these differences by changing the other person, which is what the ego naturally tries to do, but by changing your relationship to your own conditioning. Realizing that your expectations, desires, fantasies, and preferences are just your conditioning and that they are what cause you to suffer, not your partner, makes it possible to relate to that conditioning differently, to take responsibility for it and to hold it more lightly and not put it above love and the relationship. Conditioning and one's desires are not more important than love and relationship. If you give your conditioning and desires more importance than love, as the ego does, then love won't thrive within your relationship. Your demands, needs, expectations, judgments, and desires will kill the relationship.

The ego views the differences that are produced by conditioning suspiciously. It sees those who are different as wrong, bad, or inferior—which would be everybody! The ego feels justified by a sense of self-righteousness in trying to change or reform others. The ego's favorite tools of "reform," which are really ways of trying to manipulate others to get its way, are judgment, criticism, anger, bullying, threats, and withdrawal or withholding. The ego's motto in relationships is: "My way or the highway."

Such tactics are extremely damaging to relationships and have no place in relationships. Love cannot survive in such an unfriendly climate. But the ego would rather have its way than have love. Many endure or perpetuate such a hostile atmosphere and wonder why they don't feel love for their partner. But you can't expect love and judgment or other forms of unkindness to coexist. That is expecting too much.

Surrendering to Love in Relationships

It is also *accepting* too much. Judgment and other forms of unkindness are unacceptable in relationship. If you are participating in unkindness or allowing unkindness to flourish in your relationship, then you are accepting too much. You are not holding your relationship to a high enough standard. By all means accept differences, but do not accept judgment or unkindness, and don't contribute to it yourself.

If judgment and other unkind words or acts are going on in your relationship, then it is only a matter of time before the relationship ends or is declared "loveless." Judgment, criticism, anger, blame, and unkindness must be surrendered to love, or love will die.

Under those conditions love will die because you will no longer trust or feel safe with each other. Love requires trust and safety, because without these, you cannot relax. If you can't relax with your partner, you won't be able to experience your true self and therefore love. You will remain on guard, and what remains on guard is the ego. If, in your relationship, trust has been eroded, experiencing your partner from anything other than the ego will be difficult.

Relaxation and trust allow you to move out of the fearful world of the ego into the peace and love of the true self. For becoming established in a state of relaxation, safety, and peace, meditation is extremely helpful. Meditation is the bridge between the false self's world and the true self's. The more you travel this bridge in meditation, the easier it will be to travel it in the midst of your busy life and in the presence of any conflict in your relationship. Without this ability to move out of the ego and the willingness to relinquish the ego's weapons, resolving conflicts and differences in your relationships will continue to be very challenging.

The only solution to your ego (which is the only ego you are responsible for) is to find that which lies within you that does not judge but accepts differences and allows others to be as they are. The true self loves others as they are and lets them be as they are. The true self accepts the partner's differences, quirks, and imperfections, just as you would hope your partner would do for you. The true self lives and lets live, as long as the partner's behavior is not abusive or destructive, in which case your true self would have you leave the relationship.

Wouldn't it be easy to love someone who let you be as you are, who accepted you just the way you are, without trying to change you or even wanting you to be different? Are you willing to give the same acceptance and freedom to your partner? Are you willing to allow your partner to live his or her life as he or she sees fit and make his or her mistakes and learn from them? Isn't that also the freedom you want and need? This is love. This is the acceptance that every human being craves and deserves. When people accept each other and give each other the freedom to be as they are and as they choose to be, love flows between them.

If something your partner is doing grates against your conditioning or disappoints you, then you need to look at your conditioning and surrender that rather than try to change the other person's conditioning. It is not your job to change other people; it is your job to love them.

Often surrender (love) requires letting go of a desire or a fantasy: the desire for your partner to be better looking, richer, stronger, more intelligent, younger, more masculine, more feminine, thinner, more voluptuous, more muscular, neater, more organized, more responsible, more adventuresome, more exciting.... These are some of the things the ego values and desires, many of which show up in its fantasies.

These desires are quite superficial but important to the ego. All egos have such desires. Any desire you have for these things is not unique—or meaningful. Such desires are just your programming, how you have been conditioned to think and feel. They have nothing to do with your capacity to love someone, nor are they indicators of people you are best suited to be with.

Many hold their desires for their partner to be different secretly, without telling their partner of their dissatisfaction. Although that is preferable to sharing your dissatisfactions with your partner, keeping them to yourself is not the same as surrendering them. Unless you actually surrender your desires for your partner to be different, they are likely to interfere with your ability to love your partner.

Desires, such as the ego has, lead to a sense of disappointment and dissatisfaction and often to withdrawal or withholding of love. "If only he (or she) were more..., then I would be so in love!" The bad news (the reality) is that your partner will never become what you want him or her to be. But the good news is that your partner doesn't have to for you to have a loving relationship. You only have to see that your desires are no reason to withhold your love from your partner.

When you don't withhold your love, you feel love and you feel happy. That is the magic of love: It resides in you, and you feel it when you are willing to give it. The ego holds love back, as if love were a bargaining chip: "I'll love you if...." But doing that only makes you the loser. You lose the opportunity to feel love. You are the one who controls how much love you feel in a relationship: When you love, you feel love. It is a choice to love and a choice to withhold it, although often an unconscious one.

Become conscious of the ways you may be withholding love from your partner because your ego finds him or her unworthy of it or because, on some level, you feel you gain something by withholding love: Power? Control? Superiority? Safety? What is it you think you gain in holding back your love, in not jumping into your relationship with both feet? Are you angry at your partner for not doing or being something you want him or her to be, and are you withholding love to punish your partner or to try to get your partner to do what you want?

The person in front of you is the person that life has given you to love. You chose this person out of all the people that life presented you with. You can choose to give that person love or try to find another. But to choose to stay with someone and not love him or her doesn't make much sense, except perhaps to the ego, which often stays in a loveless relationship out of fear or a desire for security.

So, then the question becomes, "How do I surrender my desires for my partner to be different?" If this sounds difficult, that is only because the ego believes that its desires are really important and that it *needs* the partner to fit a certain image or fantasy in order to be happy—which is true of the ego, but not of the true self, which is what loves. To love, you have to set the ego's perceptions aside and look through different eyes, the eyes of something that *does* know how to love. You surrender the ego's perceptions for love, in order *to* love.

To the ego, surrendering desires sounds difficult (and why would it want to?), but doing this is not actually difficult. All that needs to be surrendered are thoughts. Desires, fantasies, and everything else the ego holds dear are just ideas. How difficult is it to let go of an idea? Don't you do this all the time? Thoughts arise, desires arise, and you often disregard them. You know how to do this. You already practice this daily with some thoughts.

Desires are essentially the thought "I want." If a desire has been thought about a lot, it also has a feeling component, but it stems from a thought. Is it so difficult to disregard that thought? It is difficult if you aren't aware of that thought. If you aren't aware that you are withholding love because of a desire, then you first have to become conscious of that desire and the importance you have given it. Then, once you see how empty and false that desire is, how it undermines love, and how unimportant it is in relation to the true goal, which is love, then surrendering that desire becomes easier.

Stories and images of the partner may also need to be surrendered, not only desires. With any desire, there is probably a story you tell yourself or an image you hold of your partner. For instance, if you wish your partner were physically stronger and more muscular, you might tell yourself a story something like this: "He's weak, not masculine, not sexy, so I don't feel attracted to him." And then you have a mental image that goes along with that of him being weak and unattractive. You see him a certain way in your mind's eye, which can be quite different than reality, because the mind distorts and leaves out much of reality.

When you look at him, you overlay that story and image onto him and see him through that lens. You don't actually see him, the whole of him. You aren't seeing what you love about him and what you *are* attracted to. You aren't seeing his good qualities, only what you think is lacking. You are focusing only on the negatives, which is what the ego does.

If you focus on this story and image long enough over time and talk to your friends about it, then this becomes your experience of your partner—your reality—and you begin to relate to your partner differently than if you didn't have that story and image. You create the experience of "I'm not attracted to my partner. I'm not in love with him."

That unimportant fact about him, that he isn't muscular, has been made overly important (by the ego) and now overshadows other things that are true about him and that do matter in the realm of love, canceling out your feelings of love.

There are four people in every relationship: the two real people and their internal images of each other. When both people have positive images of each other, they feel good about each other. Love flows. On the other hand, when one or both are holding negative images, there is usually trouble. Happy couples have consistently positive images of each other, at least consistent enough to sustain love, while unhappy couples have problematic images of each other. These images are in large part created and maintained by thoughts.

What you focus on in your thoughts about your partner either creates love or destroys love. You are very powerful that way. Your thoughts create an internal image of your partner, which produces feelings about your partner, which manifests as behavior toward your partner. Your inner reality becomes "your truth," and that affects the relationship.

If you don't want the reality that your thoughts, stories, and images create, then don't empower those thoughts with your attention. Instead, turn your attention onto what you love and are grateful for about your partner. Talk to your friends about that, if you must say anything, and be sure to express what you are grateful for to your partner.

It is easy to find fault! It is the easiest thing in the world. But if you focus on your partner's faults, you will fall out of love with your partner. If you focus on your partner's good qualities, you will stay in love with your partner. Your attention is that powerful. You create love and you destroy it.

So, love requires surrendering not only your desires for your partner to be different, but also your negative stories and images of your partner. As with all surrender, all you really need is the *willingness* to surrender, and the Father does the rest. So, give the ego's desires, negative stories, and images to the Father. Lay them at His feet, and He will release you from them. This giving them to the Father involves having an intention for His help and then not touching these thoughts when they arise, both of which take no time or effort whatsoever.

When these destructive desires and negative stories and images arise in your mind, notice them, recognize that they belong to the ego, and lay them at the Father's feet. Do not touch them. You don't need to have your ego's desires met to be happy or to feel love. And you don't need to destroy your relationship with a story or an image.

Then once your egoic desires and negative stories and images have been surrendered, if there remains a flame of love between you and your partner that can be fanned, it is up to you to do that. Sometimes people find that they aren't actually a match for or in love with their partner. Perhaps the love that was once there has been irretrievably destroyed or maybe it was never there to begin with.

When a relationship is founded on the things the ego values, there often isn't enough to sustain the relationship long term. Many people fall in love with an idea or image of someone, and when that person fails to live up to that, they cling to the hope that he or she will somehow become that image, or they continue to try to manipulate that person to fit that image. When false hope and manipulation, both tactics of the ego, are given up, two people might not be left with much on which to base a relationship. On the other hand, they might be left with a greater possibility for love than ever.

Love is a great mystery! What is that force that brings two people together? Sometimes it is mere physical attraction: Each person's internal images of the perfect partner are personified in each other, so they fall in love. But sometimes there is something much more than that present—true love—that gives meaning, purpose, and longevity to a relationship. You love the person's soul—who he or she *really* is, on a deep level. You love that person's *being,* and you can't imagine life without him or her. You are partners in life and supports for each other. What a blessing it is to find such a love!

Even those strong matches need to be nourished with positive thoughts and gratitude day by day, or the relationship may wither. Even in the best of relationships, you have to watch your thoughts! At any time, the ego's need to be right can rear its ugly head, and before you know it, you have traded being right for being loving.

People think they need their desires, fantasies, and expectations to be met to be happy and to be in love, but they don't! They place the responsibility for their happiness on someone else, on conditions outside themselves: "I will be happy when he (or she)...." Instead of realizing that their happiness is their responsibility and in their own hands, they think it is someone else's responsibility and in someone else's hands.

The ego's strategy for happiness is to try to get other people to behave a certain way, look a certain way, or do things a certain way. "If only I could get the world to comply with my desires, I would be happy, and *then* I will be loving." That is the ego's excuse for not being happy or loving *now*.

But there is no excuse for not being happy and not being loving now. It is your responsibility to be happy and to be loving, and this is something in life you *can* control. You can't control other people or most circumstances, but you can control your internal state. *You* make *you* happy, and only you can.

The beauty of this is that when you are happy and not making demands on others for your happiness, others find you irresistibly lovable. A happy and loving internal state creates a happy and loving external reality. You get what you want—happiness and love—by *being* what you want the other person to be: happy and loving.

If you want love in your life, you have to give love. There is no way around it! It is a natural law: Love attracts more of the same. Of course, the opposite is true: Judgment and unkindness attract judgment and unkindness. If you don't want judgment and unkindness in your relationships, then eliminate them within yourself.

The ego blames others for its unhappiness, when, in fact, it creates its own unhappiness. The ego creates a negative internal state. Then instead of taking responsibility for that, it blames others: "You made me angry! If it weren't for you, I'd be happy. You are the cause of all my problems. You don't love me enough." The truth is that your thoughts made you angry. If it weren't for your thoughts, you'd be happy. Your thoughts are the cause of all your problems. Your ego doesn't love others enough.

Your partner is not responsible for making you happy. Blaming others keeps you from realizing that you have the power to love and make yourself happy. Blaming also hurts others unnecessarily. Of course, that is the ego's intent. It is the ego's way of asserting its superiority and power. Blaming, like judging, has no place in relationships. Besides, blame is never true. It leaves out too much of the story.

Having said all this, I don't mean to imply that you can be happy and in love with just anyone. That is too much to expect. Although one's attitude makes a tremendous difference in how you experience any relationship you are in, you aren't meant to be with just anyone. The true love I am speaking about comes rarely in one's life. It takes a special combination of people, and those two people have to continue to nurture that gift of love.

The point I am making in this chapter is that to make the most of any relationship, the ego must be put aside. Some of those relationships will be passing and some will last, and all serve a purpose in your overall growth and evolution. The degree to which your relationships will be satisfying is the degree to which you are able to set aside your judgments, egoic desires, demands, expectations, and fantasies and simply *be* with the person in front of you, stripped of those, and see him or her through the eyes of love.

When you take responsibility for your own happiness and for all the ways that your conditioning interferes with your happiness, then it is possible to have a truly healthy relationship, one in which two happy people join together out of mutual love and celebration, not out of need or dependency. So, what does a healthy relationship between two happy people look like?

- ❖ You accept that sometimes your partner will judge, get angry, or behave unkindly, but you don't judge, get angry or behave unkindly in retaliation. Instead, you take a few deep breaths, relax, stay present, listen, and respond compassionately. You notice any egoic thoughts, but you surrender them as soon as they arise and keep your attention in the present moment.

- ❖ When you catch yourself judging, feeling angry, or behaving unkindly, you stop, take a few deep breaths, relax, move out of your mind and emotions, feel your body, experience what you are sensing, have compassion for yourself, forgive yourself, and then say you are sorry and ask your partner for forgiveness. This whole process may take some time.

- ❖ If you are irritated or upset by something your partner did or didn't do, you look into your own thoughts and see how you created those feelings of irritation or upset by having certain expectations or desires. You remind yourself that your partner's purpose is not to live up to or fulfill your expectations and desires. You surrender your desires or fulfill them yourself or in some other way.

- ❖ You have fun together. You play together. You laugh together. You find things that give you both pleasure and regularly do those things together. Your love is nourished by dropping into that place of joy together.

- ❖ You are relaxed and comfortable around each other. You feel like you can just be yourself, without being self-conscious or concerned about how you look or how your partner might judge you.

- ❖ You have separate interests that you each enjoy apart from each other, and you let each other have those interests. You support each other in doing whatever makes your heart sing. Your partner's cup of tea might not be your cup of tea, but it doesn't have to be. You don't have to be the same. Differences are good and appreciated for the richness they bring to the relationship.

- ❖ You practice seeing the good in your partner and noticing all the little things he or she does that contribute to your mutual well-being. You notice what you are grateful for about your partner and express your gratitude to your partner regularly for the gift that he or she is to you.

- ❖ When you disagree with your partner about something practical, like who does what around the house, you calmly state what you would like to have happen, listen to your partner's viewpoint, and then decide together how to resolve the issue so that you are both happy. Trading something for something else might be part of that solution: You do something your partner wants in exchange for your partner doing something you want. Or you do something that your partner doesn't like doing but you don't mind doing in exchange for something you don't like doing but your partner doesn't mind doing.

A chapter about love would not be complete without addressing more fully the importance of forgiveness in relationship.

Everyone makes mistakes and is hurtful sometimes, and your partner's mistakes and offenses need to be forgiven, just as yours do.

The ego keeps a tally of every hurt and offense and everything the partner didn't do that he or she was expected to do. When the tally mounts up, the ego exacts its payment through demands, anger, or withholding. This only increases the pain in a relationship, often resulting in the other person retaliating or withholding. Forgiveness sets the scale back to zero so that the relationship can pull itself out of this downward spiral and have a fresh start.

Without forgiveness, resentments and anger pile up and kill love. A lack of forgiveness keeps you focused on the partner's failing or fault or on some incident. It keeps you in the grip of your emotions and at odds with love. Without forgiveness, your ego remains in power in your consciousness, and it will continue to judge the partner and look for further justification for its anger and resentment.

The ego wants to be right, and it wants to see itself as superior. Any failings, faults, or mistakes of the partner are occasions for the ego to puff up, judge, withdraw love, or in some other way punish the partner for those mistakes or failings. The ego clings to this sense of superiority, not caring about the toll it takes on the relationship, the toll it takes on love.

In an attempt to maintain its superiority and sense of being perfect, the ego hides, from itself and others, its own failings and mistakes, denying its own humanity. This is a very unhealthy situation, because compassion and forgiveness cannot easily be accessed from this place of denial and superiority.

Being ego-identified is very lonely and isolating, and to pretend to be above reproach is an impossible burden. The unconscious is bound to sabotage such an ego in some way, as has been frequently demonstrated in cases of well-known preachers being caught with prostitutes. Human fallibility cannot be denied, or it will beg to be proven.

Forgiveness wipes the slate clean so that you can begin again anew, from a place of the true self rather than the ego. Forgiveness is often required before one can move from the ego's prison to the Father's palace. You forgive yourself for allowing the ego to run you, and you forgive your partner for allowing the ego to run him or her.

From there, it is possible to feel compassion for the human condition in which you both find yourselves: You both have egos that can make a mess of your lives and your relationships. These egos are very convincing and seem so powerful at times. Moving beyond the ego's grasp is not easy! You know that, and when you can admit that, you can forgive.

Forgiving your partner for being human allows you to see the Divine in your partner, because forgiveness makes it possible to see through the eyes of the true self. Seeing what you see and experiencing what you experience through these eyes is all you have ever really wanted and what your misguided desires were trying to attain all along. Here love lies, in surrendering everything the ego holds so dear. What a paradox this human experience is, when surrendering is what frees you and delivers everything you have ever wanted.

ABOUT the AUTHOR

Gina Lake is a nondual spiritual teacher and the author of more than twenty books about awakening to one's true nature. She is also a gifted intuitive and channel with a master's degree in Counseling Psychology and over thirty years' experience supporting people in their spiritual growth. In 2012, Jesus began dictating books through her. These teachings from Jesus are based on universal truth, not on any religion.

Then in 2017, at the request of Jesus, Gina and her husband, who is also a nondual spiritual teacher, began offering Christ Consciousness Transmissions to groups online in weekly meetings and monthly intensives. These energy transmissions are a direct current of love and healing that accelerate one's spiritual evolution.

Gina's YouTube channel has over 250 messages from Jesus to listen to. Her website offers information about her books, online courses, transmissions, a free ebook, and audio and video recordings:

www.RadicalHappiness.com

Christ Consciousness Transmission (CCT) Online Weekly Meetings

Transmission is something that naturally happens from spiritual teacher to aspirant and from beings on higher dimensions to those who are willing to receive on this dimension. Transmission has been used throughout the ages to accelerate spiritual evolution and raise consciousness. In the process, emotional and sometimes physical healing also take place, as a clearing of energy blocks from the energy field is a necessary and natural part of raising consciousness.

In weekly online Zoom video meetings, Gina Lake and her husband offer Christ Consciousness transmissions. This is one of the ways that Jesus and the other Ascended Masters working with Jesus intend to raise humanity's level of consciousness. A channeled message from Jesus is given before the transmission to prepare, teach, and inspire those who are there to receive the transmission. Many report feeling a transmission come through these channeled messages as well.

The transmission takes around twenty minutes and is done in silence except for some music, which is meant to help people open and receive. During the transmission, Gina Lake and her husband are simply acting as antennas for Christ Consciousness, as it streams to earth to be received by all who are willing to open to and be uplifted by divine grace. Since there is actually no such thing as time and space, these are not a barrier to receiving the transmission, which works as well online as in person. You can find out more about these transmissions on Gina's website at:

www.RadicalHappiness.com/transmissions

If you enjoyed this book, we think you will also enjoy these other books from Jesus by Gina Lake...

What Jesus Wants You to Know Today: About Himself, Christianity, God, the World, and Being Human: Jesus exists and has always existed to serve humanity, and one way he is doing this today is through this channel, Gina Lake, and others. In *What Jesus Wants You to Know Today*, Jesus answers many questions about his life and teachings and shares his perspective on the world. He brings his message of love, once again, to the world and corrects the record by detailing the ways that Christianity has distorted his teachings. He wants you to know that you, too, have the potential to be a Christ, to be enlightened as he was, and he explains how this is possible.

In the World but Not of It: New Teachings from Jesus on Embodying the Divine: From the Introduction, by Jesus: "What I have come to teach now is that you can embody love, as I did. You can become Christ within this human life and learn to embody all that is good within you. I came to show you the beauty of your own soul and what is possible as a human. I came to show you that it is possible to be both human and divine, to be love incarnate. You are equally both. You walk with one foot in the world of form and another in the Formless. This mysterious duality within your being is what this book is about." This book is another in a series of books dictated to Gina Lake by Jesus.

Awakening Now Online Course

It's time to start living what you've been reading about. Are you interested in delving more deeply into the teachings in Gina Lake's books, receiving ongoing support for waking up, and experiencing the power of Christ Consciousness transmissions? You'll find that and much more in the Awakening Now online course:

This course was created for your awakening. The methods presented are powerful companions on the path to enlightenment and true happiness. Awakening Now will help you experience life through fresh eyes and discover the delight of truly being alive. This 100-day inner workout is packed with both time-honored and original practices that will pull the rug out from under your ego and wake you up. You'll immerse yourself in materials, practices, guided meditations, and inquiries that will transform your consciousness. And in video webinars, you'll receive transmissions of Christ Consciousness, which are a direct current of love and healing that will accelerate your evolution and help you break through to a new level of being. By the end of 100 days, you will have developed new habits and ways of being that will result in being more richly alive and present and greater joy and equanimity.

www.RadicalHappiness.com/online-courses

More Books by Gina Lake

Available in paperback, ebook, and audiobook formats.

A Heroic Life: New Teachings from Jesus on the Human Journey. The hero's journey — this human life — is a search for the greatest treasure of all: the gifts of your true nature. These gifts are your birthright, but they have been hidden from you, kept from you by the dragon: the ego. These gifts are the wisdom, love, peace, courage, strength, and joy that reside at your core. *A Heroic Life* shows you how to overcome the ego's false beliefs and face the ego's fears. It provides you with both a perspective and a map to help you successfully and happily navigate life's challenges and live heroically. This book is another in a series of books dictated to Gina Lake by Jesus.

Jesus Speaking Series: In this series of four channeled audiobooks/books by Jesus, narrated by Gina Lake, Jesus speaks to us from another dimension to awaken Christ Consciousness within us. In this series, Jesus shows us how we can become more Christ-like and live as he did. These are nondual (Oneness) teachings and not based on any religion. Jesus explains:

> *"I am speaking to you now through this channel to help you to know of my presence and feel my presence in your life more fully. My intention is to help you realize your true nature and to live as the best human being you can be. Allow me to be your guide back home to love."*

What Jesus Wants You to Know Today: About Himself, Christianity, God, the World, and Being Human: Jesus exists and has always existed to serve humanity, and one way he is doing this today is through this channel, Gina Lake, and others. In *What Jesus Wants You to Know Today,* Jesus answers many questions about his life and teachings and shares his perspective on the world. He brings his message of love, once again, to the world and corrects the record by detailing the ways that Christianity has distorted his teachings. He wants you to know that you, too, have the potential to be a Christ, to be enlightened as he was, and he explains how this is possible.

From Stress to Stillness: Tools for Inner Peace. Most stress is created by how we think about things. *From Stress to Stillness* will help you to examine what you are thinking and change your relationship to your thoughts so that they no longer result in stress. Drawing from the wisdom traditions, psychology, New Thought, and the author's own experience as a spiritual teacher and counselor, *From Stress to Stillness* offers many practices and suggestions that will lead to greater peace and equanimity, even in a busy and stress-filled world.

In the World but Not of It: New Teachings from Jesus on Embodying the Divine: From the Introduction, by Jesus: "What I have come to teach now is that you can embody love, as I did. You can learn to embody all that is good within you. I came to show you the beauty of your own soul and what is possible as a human. I came to show you that it is possible to be both human and divine, to be love incarnate. You walk with one foot in the world of form and another in the Formless. This mysterious duality within your being is what this book is about." This book is another in a series of books dictated to Gina Lake by Jesus.

All Grace: New Teachings from Jesus on the Truth About Life. Grace is the mysterious and unseen movement of God upon creation, which is motivated by love and indistinct from love. *All Grace* was given to Gina Lake by Jesus and represents his wisdom and understanding of life. It is about the magnificent and incomprehensible force behind life, which created life, sustains it, and operates within it as you and me and all of creation. *All Grace* is full of profound and life-changing truth.

Awakening Love: How to Love Your Neighbor as Yourself: "This book is what I would teach about love if I were walking among you today. It takes its organization from particular quotes of mine and others from the Bible, which have come down through time. The quotes this book is built upon are the core teachings I gave then and I offer you today. If they are adhered to, they will change your life and change your world." –Jesus

The Jesus Trilogy. In this trilogy by Jesus, are three jewels, each shining in its own way and illuminating the same truth: You are not only human but divine, and you are meant to flourish and love one another. In words that are for today, Jesus speaks intimately and directly to the reader of the secrets to peace, love, and happiness. He explains the deepest of all mysteries: who you are and how you can live as he taught long ago. The three books in *The Jesus Trilogy* were dictated to Gina Lake by Jesus and include *Choice and Will, Love and Surrender,* and *Beliefs, Emotions, and the Creation of Reality.* Each of the books in the trilogy is also available individually and can be read in any order.

Faith, Facts, and Fiction: Finding Your Way on the Spiritual Path. In this channeled book by Jesus, he explains the ways people fool themselves and are fooled on the spiritual path and corrects many of the misunderstandings that many seekers have. How do you sort fact from fiction, faith from blind faith, and Truth from illusion? What's the truth about conspiracy theories, cults, Christianity, channeling, psychic abilities, awakening, and enlightenment? The answers are here.

Cycles of the Soul: Life, Death, and Beyond. What is the soul? And what is this human life all about? What happens at death and after death? What is it like in the afterlife, and do you plan your life before you are born? In this channeled book from Jesus, he answers these and many other questions. This wise and compassionate perspective from Jesus will help you embrace life and be at peace with life and with death.

Choosing Love: Moving from Ego to Essence in Relationships. Having a truly meaningful relationship requires choosing love over your conditioning: your ideas, fantasies, desires, images, and beliefs. *Choosing Love* describes how to move beyond judgment, anger, romantic illusions, and differences to love and oneness with another. It explains how to drop into your Being, where Oneness and love exist, and be with others from there.

For more information, please visit the "Books" page at
www.RadicalHappiness.com

Made in United States
North Haven, CT
18 July 2024